HEARING
GOD

BY BENJAMIN DIXON

Generation Culture Transformation
Specializing in publishing for generation culture change

eGenCo. LLC
824 Tallow Hill Road
Chambersburg, PA 17202, USA
Phone: 717-461-3436
Email: info@egen.co
Website: www.egen.co

 facebook.com/egenbooks

 youtube.com/egenpub

 egen.co/blog

 pinterest.com/eGenDMP

 twitter.com/eGenDMP

 instagram.com/egenco_dmp

Publisher's Cataloging-in-Publication Data
Dixon, Benjamin
            Hearing God; by Benjamin Dixon.
            pages cm.
            ISBN: 978-1-936554-72-0 paperback
                    978-1-936554-73-7 ebook
                    978-1-936554-74-4 ebook
            1. Religion. 2. Inspirational. 3. God's voice. I. Title
                            2014933712

For Worldwide Distribution, Printed in the U.S.A.

1 2 3 4 5 6 7 / 19 18 17 16 15 14

ACKNOWLEDGMENTS

This book is the direct result of so many people loving, believing in, and praying for me over the last several years. Although "thank you" is not enough, I offer my thanks with the recognition that you all contributed both to this project and the many to follow, for which I am so grateful.

To my wife Brigit, you are amazing, seriously amazing, and without your constant support and hard work, this would have never happened. To my children, thank you for sharing your dad with others and understanding that the gospel requires us to give just as we have received. I love you guys.

I want to honor all of my past and present mentors who have helped ignite and nurture my love for God, study of his word, and ministry toward people. There are just too many of you to list, but I am so grateful for your influence and want you to know that the pages of this book contain pieces of your heart as well.

To my *Ignite Global Ministries* team and board—you guys are family and I am so grateful to run with you in all that God has called us to do. Thank you for your hard work and believing in the vision as we developed *Hearing God*. This is what ministry should be like!

To Mill Creek Foursquare Church—THANK YOU for everything! You have prayed for me, supported me financially, tolerated my long sermons, but most importantly you allowed me to grow within community. I wrote this book through the many experiences I shared with you in our community and I wouldn't have it any other way.

To everyone who participated in the "Hearing God" meetings in the past, thank you! You probably didn't realize that you were the test tube to bring about this final product, and truthfully neither did I at the time. All of the "Hearing God" meetings demanded a refining process that is ultimately reflected in every page of this book. Although I haven't seen many of you for some time, I miss you and think of you often.

ENDORSEMENTS

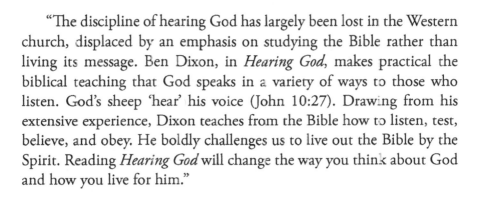

"The discipline of hearing God has largely been lost in the Western church, displaced by an emphasis on studying the Bible rather than living its message. Ben Dixon, in *Hearing God*, makes practical the biblical teaching that God speaks in a variety of ways to those who listen. God's sheep 'hear' his voice (John 10:27). Drawing from his extensive experience, Dixon teaches from the Bible how to listen, test, believe, and obey. He boldly challenges us to live out the Bible by the Spirit. Reading *Hearing God* will change the way you think about God and how you live for him."

Dave Metsker
Sr. Pastor – Crescent City Foursquare
Crescent City, CA

"Ben Dixon's *Hearing God* is stellar. How do I know? He's been ministering it among us for years now. I am privileged to serve with Pastor Ben as a shepherd in our local church and can speak to the countless (really, I lost count a long time ago) lives that have changed due to God's grace through Ben. Ben is clear and practical, taking the high idea of God speaking to each of us and making it what Jesus did: basic and elemental. He teaches a life of God-dependency through prayer. In this God-dependency, we discover the depths of relationship with God and a usefulness for his Kingdom. I can't recommend Ben's *Hearing God* enough. Everyone needs to be discipled up in this truth."

Chris Manginelli
Lead Pastor – Mill Creek Foursquare Church
Lynnwood, WA

"On many occasions believers have mentioned to me that they have a difficult time 'hearing' from God. I have often thought, 'Wouldn't it be great if there was a general resource book on this topic to give to them?' My friend, Ben Dixon, has written that book—*Hearing God*. This well-written resource is biblically sound and contains multiple examples from Ben's life as one accustomed to hearing from God on a regular basis. It is a nice blend of theology and experience. I commend to you not only this book, but also its author. Ben is a mature man of integrity, self-discipline, and a benevolent heart desirous of leading others into deeper waters of the Spirit. Ben makes hearing from God attainable for every believer, and no longer exclusively reserved on the top shelf for the highly prophetic and prophets."

Thomas P. Dooley, PhD
Author & Founder of Path Clearer Inc.
Birmingham, AL
www.pathclearer.com

"The power of this book is not simply found in its message, but the truth that all of its message is put on display in Ben's life and ministry. Everything he teaches, he lives. It's not just a message of grand ideas, but a powerful invitation of a life with Jesus that is real and centered in the scriptures. All of us can hear God's voice, sometimes we just need real help to discern how to discover this real relationship with God. This book is that help."

Phil Manginelli
Lead Pastor – The Square
Smyrna, GA

"In every generation, the Lord raises up a remnant whose heart is to transform a generation. The heart for hearing God's voice and the practical application of the prophetic gift describes who Ben is and what he does. You will find Ben's writing to be inspiring and life-transforming."

Nick Gough, MTS, DMin
Lead Pastor – Faith Center
Great Falls, MT

"Kingdom dynamics—and all good explanations of God's way— are simple. David's prayer ('God, make me know Your ways...') echoes in every heart that wants to do God's will. Ben Dixon reminds us that ministering to others in the power of the Spirit is a HUGE part of doing God's will.

As a ministry handbook, *Hearing God* is conversational, practical, and doable. You'll find yourself saying, "It can't be that simple." But it is!

If only we had more authors like Ben teaching the church about spiritual gifts and true, spiritual ministry."

Daniel A Brown, PhD
Author of *Embracing Grace* and *The Other Side of Pastoral Ministry*

"*Hearing God* is more than just a book about listening to the voice of God. It is a discipleship tool that I intend to employ. Ben possesses a rare combination of spiritual sensitivity and clear, systematic thinking. This book can take a sincere disciple through the scriptural evidence and practical application to hear God as a follower of Jesus Christ in a noisy world with lots of voices."

Rev. Crystal Guderian
Sr. Pastor of Alderwood Manor Foursquare Church
Trustee at Life Pacific College

"*Hearing God* is an excellent read. Ben Dixon gives great biblical and practical examples of hearing God's voice. God is supernatural and very practical. There is a great blend of both in this book. The book is a great training tool for those who want to grow in hearing God's voice and grow in their relationship with God. I highly recommend Ben and this book. I have had the privilege of knowing Ben and seeing his fruitful ministry in action. Get your ears ready to hear God's voice."

Dr. Dan C. Hammer
Senior Pastor – Sonrise Christian Center
Everett, Washington

"I have known Ben for many years. He carefully searches the scriptures, mining life with every encounter. Ben's passion is to go beyond head knowledge and apply scripture to the heart. With that, he does what disciplers do best: imparts, trains, and equips others to go and do likewise!

Hearing God is a great book to help Christ-followers hear the voice of God in the midst of a culture filled with sensory overload. I highly recommend this book to fine tune our spiritual ears."

Bob Hasty
Co-Senior Pastor – Rock of Roseville
www.rockofroseville.com

"I have had the privilege of experiencing God's work through Ben both directly and indirectly through the leaders he has developed around him. A number of things strike me about the amazing ministry God has given Ben. First, everything is grounded in the real and living Jesus and the written Word that he has given us. This clearly oozes out of the book. You'll encounter a man who knows Jesus and knows his Bible. Second, everything is presented in a clear, normal, everyday way. Not that Ben can't hang with the scholarly circles, but he just has a way to make hearing God extremely accessible to everyone following Jesus. Lastly, Ben is a believer in Jesus' bride, the church. What that means is no 'rogue' individuals, claiming God's voice, running around without any accountability. Rather, Ben reproduces servant leaders who want to bless his church, for the sake of his glory and Kingdom. I thank God for the gift Ben has given us here—get ready to be blessed!"

Yucan Chiu, DMin
Lead Pastor – Ethnos Community Church
www.ethnos.us

"Whether you have walked with the Lord for a long time or are a new believer, *Hearing God* is more than a place to start deepening your relationship with the Lord and practice hearing His voice. It is a good place to continue that journey and grow with sound wisdom and insight gained over years of Pastor Ben's journey to know God himself. I believe that you will enjoy this book and its stories, but most of all, I believe that you will enjoy knowing God more through your time spent in *Hearing God*."

Erik Mildes, MA
Professional Christian Counselor
Co-Founder of Seattle Christian Counseling

"Ben Dixon writes a much-needed explanation to a most common question, 'How do I hear God?' As Christians, we often use language such as 'God said,' or 'I heard from the Lord.' Ben provides not only a biblical resource on this topic, but also a sneak-peak into his personal life where hearing God is commonplace. Readers are taken on a logical journey to what, for many, is a mysterious destination... hearing God!"

Marion Ingegneri
Founding pastor – Grace Church North
National Field Director Women in Ministry Leadership, Foursquare Church, Phoenix, Arizona

---

"Far too many authors have tried writing about what they don't understand because of inexperience. Not so here. This author is experienced. This is the best I have seen written on the subject. Clear, practical, biblically sound. Follow the practical steps written in this book and you will hear God for yourself."

Herb Marks
Ministry Director – Sought Out Global
www.soughtoutglobal.com

"Ben has done a great job with this book. I not only endorse the message that Ben is teaching but also the messenger. I have witnessed Ben's effectiveness as he has trained many from my home church to hear God's voice and prophesy. Ben's life and prophetic ministry are characterized by accuracy, biblical clarity, passion, and integrity. I am excited that his years of faithful training are now put together in *Hearing God*. In this book you will get clear biblical teaching, powerful stories, and practical instruction that will give you confidence to regularly hear God's voice."

John Hammer
Author and Senior Associate Pastor – Sonrise Christian Center
isonrise.org or thefreedomletters.com (blog)

"*Hearing God* is one of the most comprehensive, biblical, practical, and easy-to-follow books regarding the incredibly important topic of how to listen to and obey God that I have come across. I not only recommend this book for spiritual enrichment, but I also recommend it for a great discipleship tool for any disciple of Jesus!"

DJ Vick
Lead Pastor – Eastside Foursquare Church
Bothell, WA

TABLE OF CONTENTS

FOREWORD

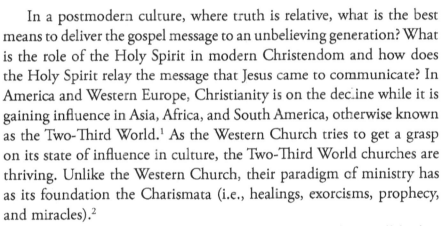

In a postmodern culture, where truth is relative, what is the best means to deliver the gospel message to an unbelieving generation? What is the role of the Holy Spirit in modern Christendom and how does the Holy Spirit relay the message that Jesus came to communicate? In America and Western Europe, Christianity is on the decline while it is gaining influence in Asia, Africa, and South America, otherwise known as the Two-Third World.[1] As the Western Church tries to get a grasp on its state of influence in culture, the Two-Third World churches are thriving. Unlike the Western Church, their paradigm of ministry has as its foundation the Charismata (i.e., healings, exorcisms, prophecy, and miracles).[2]

In America, George Barna states that, this year, there will be less than 2% of congregations who will hear a message on the Holy Spirit.[3] Asian and African theologians have complained that the American approach to church is irrelevant to Asian and African cultures.[4]

Is it possible to hear from God? It is the belief of this author that, in a postmodern culture, the apologetic is the prophetic, as Jesus demonstrates in John chapter four with a Samaritan woman of questionable repute.

Today, in order to be relevant, we need a generation that hears God's voice and knows him personally. Jon Ruthven, in his book, *What's Wrong With Protestant Theology*, says this about the message of

Jesus and the religious leaders of Jesus' time:

> The conflict between the message of Jesus and the doctrine of the religious leaders of his time (and our time) focused on the central issue of how (or if) one hears from God.... Put another way, the difference between the message of the Bible and the message of traditional (human) religion is the emphasis on two different kinds of knowing: the biblical "knowing", that is, the *experience of God*, vs. merely knowing *information about him*.[5]

Ben Dixon is a trusted leader whose teaching offers practical application on how all of us can hear the voice of God. He approaches the subject in a relational context that will draw the reader into a deeper understanding and knowledge of Jesus. Ben's humility and passion is evident to all who know him. His hunger for intimacy with Jesus will draw you into a thirst to hear the voice of God for yourself.

Nick Gough, MTS, DMin
Lead Pastor – Faith Center
Great Falls, MT

INTRODUCTION

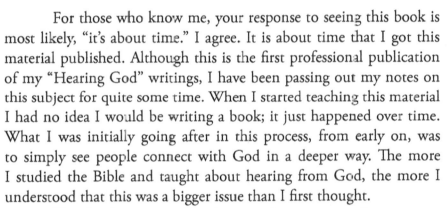

For those who know me, your response to seeing this book is most likely, "it's about time." I agree. It is about time that I got this material published. Although this is the first professional publication of my "Hearing God" writings, I have been passing out my notes on this subject for quite some time. When I started teaching this material I had no idea I would be writing a book; it just happened over time. What I was initially going after in this process, from early on, was to simply see people connect with God in a deeper way. The more I studied the Bible and taught about hearing from God, the more I understood that this was a bigger issue than I first thought.

This book is more than just words on a page. It represents dozens of classes, hundreds of students, countless revisions, and more late-night conversations than I will ever remember. After having taught on the subject of hearing God's voice for some time now, I can honestly say it has brought about some of the most effective discipleship I have ever witnessed. This discipleship has come not just from the principles in this book, but also from the drive to want people to know God, talk with God, hear from God, and ultimately respond to him in faith and trust.

I wrote this book to help people see how real God is. There are so many of us that have given our lives to Jesus Christ only to settle into a religious lifestyle rather than a loving relationship. How real are our relationships with God? Are they real enough to expect that he would talk to us? If so, what does that look like? How can I know when or if God is talking to me? Does the Bible suggest this kind of relationship for those who believe and follow Jesus? If I don't hear God, is the problem with me or with God?

Have you asked any of these questions? I sure have. Questions like these have caused me to study the Bible and seek the face of God in order to provide real answers that would lead to a deeper and more life-giving relationship with God. With great conviction and passion I submit to you my conclusions and pray that, as you read *Hearing God*, you would be inspired to wade into deeper waters of relationship, where the mystery of God's voice in your life becomes more clear than ever before.

Ben Dixon

PART I

THE FOUNDATION FOR HEARING FROM GOD

CHAPTER 1
A REAL RELATIONSHIP

At its core, Christianity is all about a relationship. Most of us have heard people describe it in this way: "Being a Christian is not about a religion; it's about a relationship." Although very true, this statement doesn't describe what a real relationship with God should look like. I became a Christian when I was 19. At the time, I would often hear pastors or other Christians say, "You can have a *personal* relationship with God through Jesus Christ. He wants you to know Him in a real way." Honestly, that invitation sounded incredible, and still does. However, when I started my walk with Jesus, I didn't fully understand what a healthy relationship looked like with a person, let alone how that should work with God. The more I heard the invitation for a "personal relationship" with Jesus the more distant I felt from God. I mean, think about it for a second. I have a lot of relationships—many of them I even call friends—but how many relationships do I have that are personal? How many people really know me, and how many people do I really know on a profoundly personal level? What about you? Did you jump into your relationship with Jesus just knowing what to do and what to expect? Of course not! I am like you. I really, really want a deep, meaningful, *personal* relationship with God, and I believe it is not only available but more importantly it's what God wants way more than we do.

My conviction is that hearing the voice of God is all about knowing God—having a personal relationship with him. It's my experience that every healthy relationship involves healthy communication, so why would this be any different in a relationship with God? I have read numerous books on the topic of hearing God and, to be honest, I have been disappointed on how seldom they focus on relationship with him. If you really want to hear God in your life then your focus must be to know him, not just to know about him. Hearing his voice is and always will be a privilege of relationship. A lot of Christianity gets sucked into a tunnel of theology and intellectualism where experience is frowned upon and knowledge is exalted. Having the right knowledge is very important, but knowing God is our goal and hearing him speak to us, for whatever reason that he does, is the outflow of a growing relationship with him. In the same way, the many aspects of hearing God that I share in this book are based on my personal relationship with him over the course of my life.

> **If you really want to hear God in your life then your focus must be to know him, not just to know about him.**

Created for Relationship

Every person on the planet at some point wonders the same thing: "Why do I exist?" Obviously we live in a time of diverse views concerning the origin and beginning of humanity, but for those of us who do believe in creationism or intelligent design, the better question is, "Why were humans created?" The Bible sheds light on this question with great clarity and leads us to a conclusion that will revolutionize our understanding and rescue us from a meaningless existence. Let's recall the creation story in the book of Genesis for a moment. In Genesis chapter 1, the Bible opens with God creating everything: the heavens, the earth, the sun, the moon, the stars, land, vegetation, animals, and last but not least, humans.

> Then God said, "Let Us make man in Our image, according to Our likeness; and let them rule over the fish of the sea and over the birds of the sky and over the cattle and over all the earth, and over every creeping thing that creeps on the earth." God created man in His own image, in the image of God He created him; male and female He created them. God blessed them; and God said to them, "Be fruitful and multiply, and fill the earth, and subdue it; and rule over the fish of the sea and over the birds of the sky and over every living thing that moves on the earth." Then God said, "Behold, I have given you every plant yielding seed that is on the surface of all the earth, and every tree which has fruit yielding seed; it shall be food for you; and to every beast of the earth and to every bird of the sky and to every thing that moves on the earth which has life, I have given every green plant for food"; and it was so. (Gen. 1:26-30)

In this brief account of human history, the first and most important part of our created purpose was to be like God (Gen. 1:26). This is not something to be taken lightly or to skip over without serious consideration. God created many awesome, wonderful, and beautiful things, but nothing was made to bear his image like us. Just think about the implications of this for a moment. Of all the things that we marvel at in creation—the sun, the stars, the earth, the mountains—you are greater and more valuable than all of them combined. Why? Because you, unlike anything else, were created to be like God and reflect his very nature. In other words, you and I are extremely special to God, his prized possession among all that he created.

We were created to be like God specifically in relationship with Him. Although all of creation *must* yield to God's voice, we have been given a greater privilege to understand, respond to, and interact with

Him. All of God's creation serves a purpose, but nothing else is able to walk with God and share life with him the way we were made to. As we consider our creation, it's important to understand that we were not made with prior knowledge of anything, but we were given the capacity to learn. The way we were made to learn was from walking out relationship with God. In the beginning, God would walk with Adam and Eve, explaining things to them, even giving them certain responsibilities that he would observe and speak into. It was beautiful. At one point God invited Adam to give names to the animals and even wanted to see what he would name them.

> Out of the ground the LORD God formed every beast
> of the field and every bird of the sky, and brought *them* to the
> man to see what he would call them; and whatever the man
> called a living creature, that was its name. (Gen. 2:19)

What a profound picture! It reminds me of family and, more specifically, of the relationship of a father and his children. I have four kids and over the years we have been able to work on many projects together. Just recently I was able to make some pinewood derby cars for my youngest kids. I cut the car out of a block of wood and sanded everything smooth, then I asked my kids to choose the color of paint and stickers to put on the car which they were so eager to do. The truth is, I made the car, but in the final stage, I invited my kids to contribute to the finished product. They were so excited to be a part of this but, to be honest, I was more excited than both of them that we could do this together. I could have done everything without them, but I wanted to see what paint color they would choose, and what crazy stickers they would put on the car to make it their own. This exemplifies relationship, and this is what we see with God and Adam in the beginning of our creation story: "and brought *them* [*animals*] to the man to see what he would call them" (Gen. 2:19). God created us for a *real* relationship, which is what hearing his voice is all about. Without understanding this truth, we will always be missing something in our experience with him—always!

A Damaged Relationship

Although we were made for relationship with God, the story of Adam and Eve also reveals the very serious problems that exist for all of us. God blessed Adam and placed him in the Garden of Eden to steward and cultivate the other things that he created.

> Then the LORD God took the man and put him into the garden of Eden to cultivate it and keep it. The Lord God commanded the man, saying, "From any tree of the garden you may eat freely; but from the tree of the knowledge of good and evil you shall not eat, for in the day that you eat from it you will surely die." (Gen. 2:15-17)

God told them that they could eat from any tree in the garden except one tree, which is referred to as the "tree of the knowledge of good and evil" (Gen 2:17). As God introduced a command of abstinence surrounding this forbidden fruit he also introduced a choice to Adam and Eve. It's hard to know how this command effected them as they would walk by the forbidden tree every day, knowing they couldn't eat its fruit, and wondering why it's even in the garden. However, all Adam and Eve knew for sure was what God said; that was their reality and outside of God speaking to them they had no knowledge in and of themselves. Knowing this about Adam and Eve makes the name of the tree even more interesting to me. The tree was called "the knowledge of good and evil" (Gen 2:17). Really? Do you see what I do? If all they knew was what God said, this tree not only introduced a choice for them, but it also introduced a new path to obtain knowledge without having to listen to God. This is where the "God's-way-or-my-way" option all began.

The introduction of the tree is a difficult concept in itself, but in Genesis chapter 3 we are introduced to another problem: the serpent. At first we have God, Adam, then Eve, and now a new character that plays an important role in our story. We know from other passages in the Bible that the serpent is none other than the devil who once was an angel and part of heaven's host, but through pride was cast out (Rev 12:9). The devil hates God, his creation, and everything that God says is good. However, he does not have authority to just do as he pleases and so we read of his trickery and deceptive ways with Adam and Eve.

> Now the serpent was more crafty than any beast of the field which the Lord God had made. And he said to the woman, "Indeed, has God said, 'You shall not eat from any tree of the garden'?" The woman said to the serpent, "From the fruit of the trees of the garden we may eat; but from the fruit of the tree which is in the middle of the garden, God has said, 'You shall not eat from it or touch it, or you will die.'" The serpent said to the woman, "You surely will not die! For God knows that in the day you eat from it your eyes will be opened, and you will be like God, knowing good and evil." When the woman saw that the tree was good for food, and that it was a delight to the eyes, and that the tree was desirable to make *one* wise, she took from its fruit and ate; and she gave also to her husband with her, and he ate. Then the eyes of both of them were opened, and they knew that they were naked; and they sewed fig leaves together and made themselves loin coverings. (Gen. 3:1-7)

Somehow the devil was aware of God's command to abstain from this tree, and as an enemy of God sought to deceive Adam and Eve. The first thing the devil did was question what God had told them by opposing the very voice of God to them: "has God said?" Although Eve reiterated God's command back to the devil, he did not stop with his temptation, but actually pressed all the more. The devil tried to convince Eve, and ultimately Adam, that if they ate the fruit nothing bad would happen, but rather they would "be like God' in that they would "know" good and evil. What the devil did not say, and Adam and Eve did not remember, was that they were already created to be like God. Therefore, their temptation was to become "like God" without having a relationship with God. The Lord surely wanted Adam and Eve to be like Him, but not autonomously, not apart from his voice and his teaching through daily relationship.

Ultimately, we know that Adam and Eve listened to the devil's voice and ate from the tree of the knowledge of good and evil. This choice brought about serious consequences that has effected every generation since. God told them that if they ate the tree they would "die" (Gen 2:17). Now we know as the story goes on that they did not physically die right then and there, so what did God mean when he said they would die? He meant that they would die spiritually and, with that, their relationship with him would be damaged and in need of serious repair. This moment is commonly referred to as "the Fall" and rightly so, for we truly fell from something beautiful: a close relationship with God. This is where things became complicated for humanity. Every person born after Adam and Eve enters into an identity crisis, in which we long for relationship with God, to hear him and follow his voice, but are held back by our desire to love ourselves and to follow our own way which is rooted in listening to the devil. But God did not sit back and allow us to go our own way without putting a plan into motion that could restore the damaged relationship.

Jesus Came to Restore

Many things transpired from the time of Adam and Eve to the moment when Jesus stepped into our world. Although God knew how damaged our relationship with him was, that does not mean that we necessarily did. In time, the Lord chose to reveal his ways through the giving of the law, which of course came through Moses. In God's law, both the Ten Commandments and the many other regulations found in the Torah, we were given communication from God on what to do and how to do it. The people of that day were unable to fully keep these laws so God introduced additional systems whereby they could approach Him and maintain some level of relationship. These systems were the temple (the place of God's presence), the priests (the ministers that mediated between God and humankind), and the sacrifices (the way that humans could atone for their sins and be right with God again). If a person sinned he could bring an animal sacrifice to the temple and a priest would sacrifice the animal in order to atone for the sins of that person and his family. In the Old Testament, this was the way one lived before God and this was the kind of relationship available to individuals. It doesn't exactly sound like what we were made for, nor does it look like a real relationship at all. Surely this isn't what God wanted with us: a law, a system, distance?

However different the Law was from the real relationship that we were created to have with God, it still played a very important role in our history. The Apostle Paul explains in his letter to the Galatians why the Law was given.

> Why the Law then? It was added *because of transgressions*, having been ordained through angels by the agency of a mediator, *until the seed would come* to whom the promise had been made. (Gal. 3:19)

In this letter Paul clearly explains that the Law was meant to reveal that we could not produce righteousness and at the same time we could not restrain unrighteousness in our choices and lifestyle. This predicament was the result of eating from the tree of the knowledge of good and evil. From our current vantage point in history, we see clearly the far-reaching consequences of listening to the devil and ourselves instead of to God. The Law was given to reveal what sin had become in our lives and how we truly needed a savior to bring us back to a real relationship with God. To that end, Jesus came. "For the Son of Man has come to seek and to save that which was lost" (Luke 19:10).

Jesus said he "came to seek and save that which was lost" at the tail end of a conversation with a sinful man who was despised by his whole community. Once again, we ask, "What was lost?" We obviously know that we had become lost, but I think this could be expanded a bit to speak directly to what we lost. We lost our relationship with God. We lost our connection to his voice, in real time, and in real ways.

The word "lost" in this passage can mean "destroy" or even "damage." When we chose to listen to another voice, relationship with God was damaged, but Jesus came with the remedy to set all things right. "But now in Christ Jesus you who formerly were far off have been brought near by the blood of Christ" (Eph. 2:13).

In the Old Testament, people would bring a sacrifice to God so their sins could be forgiven and fellowship with God could be restored. Such restoration was always temporary. In the New Testament, God the Father sent his son Jesus to be a perfect once-and-for-all sacrifice so that our relationship with him would be permanently reconnected. All we need to do is believe! Believe what? Believe that what Jesus did is enough! His death, burial, and resurrection is the only thing that can bring us close to God, nothing else. The only way to the Father is through the Son, and the only way to Jesus is to believe what he did for you. This is all we bring to the table for our relationship with him to be reconnected. We were far off in our sin, but in Jesus Christ we are brought close enough to know God and thus close enough to hear him again. In our choice to sin we damaged the very relationship we were made for, but in Jesus' choice to give his life, we can be restored to his loving care once again.

God loves us so much that he spared no expense to bring us back into the kind of relationship he created us for. The death, burial, and resurrection of Jesus Christ is God's way of eternally saying to us, "*I love you.*" If you ever wonder whether God loves you or not, you only need to remember the cross and the blood that was shed for you. He did for us what we could never do for ourselves because he wanted us more than we wanted him. This is God. This is love. Jesus shared his heart with his disciples in a way that shows the kind of relationship we have been talking about.

> Truly, truly, I say to you, he who does not enter by the door into the fold of the sheep, but climbs up some other way, he is a thief and a robber. But he who enters by the door is a shepherd of the sheep. To him the doorkeeper opens, and the sheep hear his voice, and he calls his own sheep by name and leads them out. When he puts forth all his own, he goes ahead of them, and the

sheep follow him because they know his voice. A stranger they simply will not follow, but will flee from him, because they do not know the voice of strangers. (John 10:1-5)

This sermon from Jesus grew out of his confrontation with Jewish leaders after they excommunicated a beggar that Jesus healed (John 9). Jesus begins to talk about who he is and what God is really like, in contrast to the example of the religious leaders who were stealing the correct view of God from the people. Jesus refers to himself as the Shepherd and his followers as the sheep. He says, "he [Jesus] calls his own sheep by name!" (John 10:3) Think about this for a moment. Our name is the most personal thing that we have as it defines who we are and even who our family is. Jesus not only knows us

The devil knows our names and calls us by our sin, but the Lord knows our sin and calls us by our names.

by name but he calls us with the singular goal that we might follow him wherever he goes. The devil knows our names and calls us by our sin, but the Lord knows our sin and calls us by our names. Who do we really want to listen to? We were not made to follow a stranger's voice, the devil's voice, or our own voice, but every person was made to hear and follow their Shepherd's voice. My friends, he is calling *your* name. "My sheep hear My voice, and I know them, and they follow Me" (John 10:27).

As we give our lives to Jesus, he opens our ears to hear him and even more importantly, to follow him again so that we can become what he originally made us to be through our relationship with him.

Your Father

As we look at the life of Jesus, it's extremely important to know that he not only came to be our Savior, but He also came to be our Pattern. Jesus exemplified a life with God that in every way is the pattern for what our lives with God could and should be like. Although Jesus was the busiest person on the planet, he always prioritized his relationship with God, which we see clearly in his frequent travels to the mountains for all-night prayer. The religious leaders of that day lived by a system, while Jesus lived by a relationship. That isn't to say that the system the religious leaders lived by was entirely wrong in its essence, but we must note that Jesus was revealing something new, primarily for our sake, in the way he lived life with God while on earth.

When Jesus came, he referred to God as his father. This was not the kind of relationship that anyone had with God at this time. It actually made the religious leaders angry that Jesus would freely speak of God in this way. As we read the gospel accounts in the Bible, we find that Jesus not only referred to God as his father, but also as *our* Father. During the Sermon on the Mount, Jesus referred to God as *our* Father over 15 times. Jesus was speaking prophetically regarding the nature of relationship he was about to establish between God and man, through his sacrifice. Those who trust in Jesus are adopted into God's family and are forever called to experience his love as their Father. It's amazing to know that God wants a relationship

> **Those who trust in Jesus are adopted into God's family and are forever called to experience his love as their Father.**

with us, but the kind of relationship that he is offering blows my mind. God wants to be *our* Father! Look at these references as we consider this radical invitation.

> [N]or does *anyone* light a lamp and put it under a basket, but on the lampstand, and it gives light to all who are in the house. Let your light shine before men in such a way that they may see your good works, and glorify *your Father* who is in heaven. (Matt. 5:15-16)

> But I say to you, love your enemies and pray for those who persecute you, so that you may be sons of *your Father* who is in heaven; for He causes His sun to rise on *the* evil and *the* good, and sends rain on *the* righteous and *the* unrighteous. (Matt. 5:44-45)

> Therefore you are to be perfect, as *your heavenly Father* is perfect. (Matt. 5:48)

> He said to them, "When you pray, say: '*Father*, hallowed be your name. Your kingdom come.'" (Luke 11:2)

These are merely a few of the references in which Jesus proclaims to those who would hear it, "God wants to be *your* Father!" It seems to me that most Christians struggle to understand what their relationship with God is really suppose to look like, and these are feelings that have been very real for me as well. But as we look at the words of Jesus, he makes it very plain as to what our relationship with God is supposed to be like. He didn't stop with a simple description; instead, Jesus lived it out in front of us so we could actually see how this works. The good news of Jesus is not so much about what we are saved from, which is noteworthy, but it really is all about what we are saved *for*—a father-son (or -daughter) relationship with God Almighty. If that doesn't make you get up and shout then I am afraid to say that nothing will!

As we continue to look at the issue of hearing God through the lens of relationship, we must know that God will always speak to us as the loving Father that he is. Everything that we think God is saying to us must be filtered through how a loving father would speak to his child. This focal point will lay the foundation for hearing him more clearly in our lives. This is something that took me a long time to learn but has helped me more than anything else in my relationship with God with regard to hearing his voice. Look at what the Father says to Jesus after he was baptized by John in the Jordan River: "... and a voice came out of heaven, 'You are My beloved Son, in You I am well-pleased'" (Luke

3:22). At this point Jesus had not healed anybody, he wasn't traveling around preaching the Kingdom, nor was he performing miracles for the multitude. He was just living in sonship and God was pleased with him. A loving father speaks to you based on relationship (who you are), not on performance (what you do).

A loving father speaks to you based on relationship (who you are), not on performance (what you do).

When we are in Christ, we too will hear God affirm our identities and proclaim his pleasure over us, which is always the basis for everything else he will ever say to us.

I grew up in a Christian home with a good mother and father who loved and cared for me. We were not without problems, but I knew my dad loved me by what he said and the things that he did. My relationship with my dad is better now than it has ever been and when we talk, regardless of what it's about, I know the things that he says are motivated by his love for me as his son. The relationship I have with my dad has helped me see God the right way; now I am raising my kids as it was modeled to me. In the same way, God designed the family to be a model of what relationships in heaven are going to be like, and ultimately to prepare us to relate to him and one another as our true eternal family. Many of us have not experienced much good from our family relationships, so in a sense we have been robbed by our bad examples. This damage lingers in our souls until the Lord heals our pain through relationship with Him.

Some of us never heard "I love you" or "I am proud of you" in our family experience. Many of us were pressured by a performance-based relationship with our parents in which expectations were unrealistic. These examples have made it difficult for us to receive God's love and hear him speak to us as Father, which has caused our relationships with him to suffer. If that is true of you, there is good news. God can and will heal your pain because he is "a father of the fatherless" (Ps. 68:5) and a mender of broken hearts. As you seek to hear God's voice, be sure of this: before he wants to tell you what to do or congratulate your obedience, he wants you to know that in Christ "you are [his] beloved child and in you [he is] well pleased" (Luke 3:22).

Remember, how we perceive God is most often the lens through which we hear God, or at least interpret what he says to us. If we think of God as an angry taskmaster then when we read the Bible or hear a word from the Holy Spirit, we will tend to hear something like this at the foundation of that word: "You better do this *or else!*" This is not at all how God wants to be toward us. But when you think of God as Jesus revealed him—a loving Father—you will hear something like this at the foundation of everything he says to you: "This is what is best for you, so I need you to trust me on this."

One evening my wife and I were watching a Christian documentary on the influence of music. The main speaker throughout the film made some incredibly good points about how powerful music is and how most Christians don't realize what they are allowing into their lives, in a spiritual sense, when they listen to music. I was challenged by the speaker's perspective and extensive amount of research that this team had pulled together to help Christians wholeheartedly honor the Lord in what they listen to. The documentary was filmed at a large church, and as it came to a close, the main speaker began to share with the people that God spoke to him several days before this event. He began to talk about his encounter with God and then said that God told him to tell everybody, "If you don't repent and get the idols of this music out of your lives, then he will remove his Holy Spirit from you!" After hearing this I almost fell off my couch! "What did he just say?" I thought. I mean, I am all for challenging the family of God, but this man quoted an Old Testament scripture from King David's psalm of remorse (Ps. 51:11), and then told New Covenant believers, who are sealed with the Holy Spirit, that if they don't throw away some CDs, the Holy Spirit would leave them. Let me be clear; God did not speak to this man, and even if God was trying to speak to him, his view of God is so removed from that of a loving Father that I wonder if he actually understands God's love for him, let alone the thousands of people he is talking to.

Jesus gave his life so his Father would be ours as well. I encourage you to let that soak in and inform every thought you have about who God is and how he wants to speak to you. As we see God through the

Jesus gave his life so his Father would be ours as well.

real relationship of father-to-child he has offered us, we will hear him accurately as well.

Embracing Sonship

When I was 24 years old I married my amazing wife Brigit. As I committed myself to being her husband, I also became a step-father for two young boys that my wife brought with her into our relationship. Her boys were nine and eleven years old when we were married, and they each had different biological fathers who had not been in their lives for a long time. I had never pictured myself being a step-father before, but I sensed a God-given courage to become a father to these boys. At first we were all excited about this new relationship. My wife told me that they had prayed every night for God to bring them a father and I felt very special to be an answer to this ongoing prayer. I was optimistic. This was going to be amazing; no muss, no fuss, just smooth sailing, right? Not exactly. With time, the difficulties began to come, and to be honest, the issues we had were probably similar to that within most families, blended or not. However, I was learning how to be a father to half-grown boys that didn't have to acknowledge me as their dad if they didn't want to. That was where I started hearing something from God about my relationship with Him.

Several years into our new family dynamic, I was praying through a difficulty with one of my sons and I remember waking up with a phrase recurring in my mind: "Embrace sonship." This phrase came to me so many times I simply could not deny it was from God. I began to pray and think about what this phrase meant, especially in the context of what I was working through with my own son. As I began writing in my journal about this experience, I observed the grieving that

I was experiencing as a father and it soon just clicked! I realized that I had no issues being a father; I was committed to loving, caring for, helping, and reconciling with my sons. But I could see that my boys were struggling through embracing their sonship, specifically in the context of having a new father. To that point they had grown up with a mother, and never had a father until I came around. Even though they prayed for a dad, it didn't mean they knew how to receive from one when he came. Although I didn't really know how to be a father, I had fully embraced my role and responsibility to be one. The boys however didn't know how to be sons to a dad, so they were struggling through embracing their sonship as this relationship they seemingly wanted was thrust upon them. I think we can be much like this when we become Christians. As we figure out that God is our Father, we must also learn what it means to be his child and embrace this as our reality, our identity. As a father, I can honestly say that many of the tension points I have with my children are somehow connected to their not embracing their role as sons and instead they try and play the role of parent.

As we learn to hear from God, especially in the context of relationship, it's vital to our development that we embrace our identity as a son or daughter of God. This is who we are and this is the context in which God will both relate and speak to us. I have seen many accept that God is *God*, and maybe even carry a level of understanding that he is reaching out as a Father, but the future fruitfulness of our relationships with Him have to do with our embracing

As we learn to hear from God, especially in the context of relationship, it's vital to our development that we embrace our identity as a son or daughter of God.

of sonship more fully. There are many ways to do this, but on a practical level I started calling God "dad" in my personal prayer time. This may sound strange, and when you begin doing it you may feel odd, but this is one thing I did to embrace who God says I am—his son. This relationship with him is something you have to embrace, and to do so means it will get practical on some level. Otherwise, our religious mindsets will keep us from receiving what Jesus paid for on our behalf.

I remember when I first started teaching about hearing God's voice. We would have monthly meetings at our church and it was normal for new people to come, being invited by their friends. I remember one meeting, in which we had a young woman in attendance for her first time. She seemed fine during the teaching, but once we started praying I noticed that she got very uncomfortable. I asked someone from the audience to sit in a chair facing everybody else, while the rest of us in the room prayed and asked God to speak to us for her encouragement. The more people would share what they *thought* God might be saying to the person in the chair, the more I noticed this young woman wanting to bolt for the door. As we finished praying I closed the meeting and walked over to this woman and her friend and asked if everything was all right. She immediately said, "How can you just demand that God speak to you right now? I mean, he is God!" to which I replied, "I guess I don't see God the same way you do. I think he is a loving Father who gets excited when his kids want to know what he thinks about another person, so they can be an encouragement." I am sure that statement bounced around in her head like a pinball machine until she simply said, "Yeah, I guess you're right." What she shared with me next is the same story I hear over and over again. "I was raised in a church where it seemed all about church and very little about developing a relationship with God, especially one that would involve communication from Him—that would be crazy!" This woman did not see God as a loving Father and consequently had not embraced her own identity as his daughter, which clearly effected her ability to hear God, at least until that night!

Repentance Is the Key

Often I find that the missing element in our experience concerning hearing God's voice is primarily related to repentance. I realize that repentance can be one of those dark and dreary words, but truthfully repentance is such a gift to those who want to know God. Repentance is our response to what Jesus came to do. In fact, repentance and faith are the only re-

> **Often I find that the missing element in our experience concerning hearing God's voice is primarily related to repentance.**

sponses necessary to the work of Jesus on our behalf.

The word "repent" in the original language means to change your mind, and consequently, your actions. That's it. When you look up the word "repent" in most dictionaries (not based on the original language), you will find references about being "sorry" or being "sorry again." If your experience has been anything like mine, you have been around the old school repentance preachers that think making people feel temporarily sorry somehow leads them to change their ways. You and I know that feeling sorry about something doesn't necessarily make you change. Therefore, the essence of repentance is really about denying your way of doing things and embracing God's way of doing things; it's when you stop listening to your own voice and start listening to God's voice. When Adam and Eve disobeyed God and ate from the tree of the knowledge of good and evil, they listened to the devil's voice and began walking in what seemed right to them.

As we embrace the finished work of Jesus, we believe what He did on the cross brings forgiveness and restores us to right relationship with God. However, as we believe, we must repent from our self-willed ways and learn to hear his voice and *follow* him (John 10:27), which we walked away from many centuries ago through our disobedience toward God.

In taking a quick look at repentance as it relates to hearing God and our relationship with him, we need to see the frequency by which it was preached. Look at these passages.

John the Baptist

Now in those days John the Baptist came, preaching in the wilderness of Judea, saying, *"Repent, for the kingdom of heaven is at hand."* (Matt. 3:1-2)

Jesus

From that time Jesus began to preach and say, *"Repent, for the kingdom of heaven is at hand."* (Matt. 4:17)

Apostle Peter

Peter *said* to them, *"Repent, and each of you be baptized in the name of Jesus Christ for the forgiveness of your sins;* and you will receive the gift of the Holy Spirit." (Acts 2:38)

Repentance was the primary message of John the Baptist. Then we see the same message in the life of Jesus and his twelve disciples. What was this about? Was Jesus trying to make people feel sorry for their sins? If so, he sure came a long way to make people feel bad. Of course we know this isn't true, but Jesus was after something specific in his message of repentance. This is something that I think we often miss when we don't look at the whole picture: God created us for relationship (including daily communication), but we chose to sin and listen to another voice. Then, Jesus came to restore us back to relationship with our Father in giving his own life for us, and now he is calling us to repent and believe again. I think Christians get the believe part down, at least as it relates to trusting what Jesus did on the cross as the only way to salvation. However, the repentance piece, in my opinion, is the key that unlocks the relationship aspect of what Jesus paid for.

Jesus said, "Repent, for the kingdom of heaven is at hand" (Matt. 4:17), and then he began teaching, to everyone who would listen, about the ways of *his* kingdom. Hearing God begins with humbling ourselves and repenting from following our thoughts, our ways, and our opinions, and instead embracing God's thoughts and ways which are revealed in the Bible and through the Holy Spirit.

Remember, we were made to walk with God and believe what he says as our reality. Unfortunately, we have strayed so far from this dynamic of relationship with God that we need repentance at the foundation of our relationship with God to assure that we listen to and follow him. When Jesus was on the earth, many heard him teach, but only the ones that drew near to hear *and follow* were the ones that shared relationship with him. A person with a repentant heart is not only looking to hear from God; they are committed to following him, no matter what he might say.

A person with a repentant heart is not only looking to hear from God; they are committed to following him, no matter what he might say.

This is where we make Jesus the *Lord* in our lives and not just Savior. His lordship in our lives is the essence of coming into his kingdom. Jesus is the King and he came revealing what his kingdom is like to those who choose to enter. But entering this Kingdom means we willingly subject ourselves to the rule and will of the King, where his will is our will, and his truth is our truth, and all is well again. If you want to hear God, you will need to dethrone yourself as the sovereign ruler over your life and let King Jesus sit back on the throne of your soul.

Chapter 1 Review Questions

1. Is the relationship that you have with God truly personal? If so, what makes it personal? If not, what is it lacking?

2. In your relationship with God do you interact with him as your Father? How would your relationship with God change if you perceived him as a good father?

3. Do you believe that hearing from God is related to your relationship with Him? If so, how?

4. What encouraged you most about this chapter and how will you apply it to your life?

CHAPTER 2
HEARING GOD IS FOR EVERYONE

In our society the topic of hearing from God can be difficult to discuss, so much so that it seems like anybody who claims to hear from God is scrutinized heavily and in many cases written off completely. The media finds the strangest people who claim, "God told me to do this," and everyone reading or watching thinks, "What a crazy person." Well, yes. They probably could be crazy, in a literal sense. But the subtle message the media aims for by interviewing these kinds of people is, "Here we go again; another nut case saying that God spoke to them." While they may have reported accurately regarding that particular person, there is a cynical perspective being imparted to viewers toward *anyone* who claims to hear from God. Even Christians pick up this cynicism, especially when they have no experience with God speaking to them or to anyone they know.

This might sound like a conspiracy theory comment but I think the enemy does use mainstream media to cast a dark shadow on real Christianity. There are thousands of stories around the globe of God speaking to people, performing mighty miracles, and using people to serve others naturally and supernaturally. Who is documenting these stories? You know as well as I do that it rarely happens. But if some high-level preacher gets caught up in sexual sin you better believe they will show that story for months in multiple media formats. Listen, there is a real attack from the enemy to discredit the supernatural reality of God and his people. The fruit of this attack is widespread skepticism in the Body of Christ—brothers and sisters in Christ believing in a living God who, for some reason, never talks to people today.

If you're a Christian then you believe in a supernatural God who does supernatural things and even chooses to do them through people. In other words, if we struggle with the reality of God speaking

If you're a Christian then you believe in a supernatural God who does supernatural things and even chooses to do them through people.

to us, we need to be reminded that we serve a *living* God who is not subject to natural order, an order which He created. You can't even be a Christian unless you believe that Jesus rose from the dead! Our God is alive, and He speaks to people.

There is no place for cynicism in the heart of a Christian. Should we be discerning? *Yes!* Should we weigh the things that people say God has spoken? *Yes!* But in no way should that translate into being automatically skeptical of a real and living God talking to real and living people. While the media, non-believers, and others seek to discredit the reality of a loving God who communicates to humanity, we must resist their report and seek our counsel from the Bible.

When you study the Bible you quickly discover that the majority of individuals therein who are discussed at any length heard God speak in one way or another. It could easily be concluded that hearing from God was somewhat common for those that walked closely with the Lord. If it was common for the men and women of old, then it should be common for those who walk with the Lord today. So often we claim to believe the Bible, but what we really mean is that we believe those things happened back then, but no longer happen for us today. Be assured that the same God who spoke to people in Bible times is the same God that lives in us through the Holy Spirit today. Nothing has changed because God himself hasn't changed! "Jesus Christ *is* the same yesterday and today and forever" (Heb. 13:8).

In the last several years I have discussed the topic of hearing from God with many people. I feel like I have heard almost every perspective regarding this topic, but who knows, maybe there are others I have yet to hear. In these conversations, I have been able to convince a number of people that God speaks today as He always has. The most powerful part of someone knowing this truth occurs when that person begins to expect that God will actually speak on a personal level. Expectation will turn apathy into an honest pursuit to hear God speak. This is a game-changer for spiritual life. Our expectations fuel our faith toward God, planting within us an eager readiness to hear his voice that wasn't there before.

Expectation will turn apathy into an honest pursuit to hear God speak.

Several people that I know still don't understand text messaging and most of them have no desire to. I can send them a text message and their phones are capable of receiving my message, but I will never receive a reply from any of them. They can receive the text message but because they don't check their messages or know how to, our communication does not happen. In the same way, everyone *can* hear the voice of God, but that doesn't mean everyone *does*. Just because something is available doesn't mean we take advantage of it.

Let's assume that you or someone you know is asking the question, "Why do you believe God speaks to people today?" My answer is very simple. God spoke to the people in the Bible, God spoke to people throughout history, and God speaks to many people today. We will spend the rest of this chapter laying a foundation for the reality of God speaking to people in the past and present.

Hearing God in the Old Testament

The first time we read of God speaking to people is found in the creation account of Genesis. God created Adam and Eve and then told them what He wanted them to do.

> God blessed them; and God said to them, "Be fruitful and multiply, and fill the earth, and subdue it; and rule over the fish of the sea and over the birds of the sky and over every living thing that moves on the earth." (Gen. 1:28)

It's safe to assume that God spoke to Adam and Eve clearly, personally, and audibly. However, in Genesis chapter three, Adam and Eve chose to sin and from that moment God's interactions with them, and with men and women as a whole, began to change dramatically.

In the Old Testament we continue to read of God speaking audibly to people such as Cain and Abel, Noah, Abraham, and many others (Gen. 4:9; 7:1; 12:1). As more time goes on, God's communication toward people becomes less personal. In Genesis chapter 20 God begins to communicate to people through dreams. From that point forward in the Bible we read of a widening distance in God's relationship with humans along with an increase of various forms of communication between God and humans.

In the book of Exodus, a man named Moses has a dramatic encounter with the Lord (Exod. 3). From this encounter he is sent to deliver the nation of Israel from the bondage of slavery to Egypt and reconnect them to the God of their ancestors. The Bible reveals that God had a special relationship with Moses and communicates with him personally, which is very similar to what Adam and Eve had before they sinned. "Thus the LORD used to speak to Moses face to face, just as a man speaks to his friend…" (Exod. 33:11).

In the Old Testament there are few people that had the kind of relationship with God that Moses did. God himself said this to those who opposed Moses:

> Then the LORD came down in a pillar of cloud and stood at the doorway of the tent, and He called Aaron and Miriam. When they had both come forward, He said, "Hear now My words: If there is a prophet among you, I, the Lord, shall make Myself known to him in a vision. I shall speak with him in a dream. Not so, with My servant Moses, He is faithful in all My household; With him I speak mouth to mouth, Even openly, and not in dark sayings, And he beholds the form of the Lord. Why then were you not afraid To speak against My servant, against Moses?" (Num. 12:5-8)

While this passage reveals the close relationship that God had with Moses, it also tells us that God was not very personal in his communication with others at this time. That's important to know as we read about the various ways in which God would speak to people in the Old Testament.

Through Moses, God established his Law and even after Moses died, the Law revealed how Israel was to live. However, God still used various mediators to communicate to His people, which would help them know his priorities amidst their current circumstances. The primary mediators of God's voice in the Old Testament were prophets, priests and kings.

The word prophet means "a spokesperson," and refers to someone who acts as God's mouthpiece.[6] The Bible refers to Abraham and Moses as prophets (Gen. 20:7; Deut. 18:15), but through Samuel God began a successive line of prophetic voices that He used to speak to his people. These prophets were men like Elijah, Elisha, Jeremiah, Isaiah, and Ezekiel.

In 1 Samuel 8, the nation of Israel gathered together to demand that the Prophet Samuel appoint them a king. Up until this point Israel did not have a king like the other nations. Samuel was grieved by their request because he was jealous for Israel to have only God as their king. God granted the request of Israel and sent Samuel to appoint a man named Saul as the first king of Israel (1 Sam. 9:16). The kings of Israel became the primary mediator for the voice of God in their day. A righteous king was one who followed the Law, listened to the voice of the Lord, and led the people to do the same. An unrighteous king strayed from God's Law, ignored God's voice, and consequently led the people to do the same.

Through all this we see how God originally made humans to be close to him personally, but with Adam and Eve's sin, humanity experienced distance from God and acclimated to hearing his voice through mediators such as prophets, priests and kings. This was not God's ultimate plan but it surely served a purpose in time and history, which will help us as we continue to look at the unfolding of God's relationship and communication with humanity.

Hearing God in the Life of Jesus

The more you read the Old Testament, the easier it is to see a God who is distant that communicates through chosen people to the commonplace masses. When Jesus came to earth, the people of Israel were oppressed by the Roman government and by the religious establishment that reinforced a distant God and his specially anointed few. God broke the distance barrier by coming close to us in Jesus Christ.

God the Father sent his one and only Son to fully restore us. Jesus is the full provision of God for us and

God broke the distance barrier by coming close to us in Jesus Christ.

everything we need is found in him. As we turn to Jesus Christ, he becomes our one and only Mediator through whom God the Father will speak. Jesus is our Prophet, Priest, and King. God may use others to speak into our lives, but we can all be on a personal level with God because of Jesus.

> God, after He spoke long ago to the fathers in the prophets in many portions and in many ways, in these last days has spoken to us in His Son, whom He appointed heir of all things, through whom also He made the world. (Heb. 1:1-2)

Jesus wanted people to know and hear God, which is why he came. "My sheep hear my voice, and I know them, and they follow me" (John 10:27). Jesus not only told people that this kind of relationship was possible, but he gave his life to make it available. That is good news!

Hearing God through the Holy Spirit

After walking with his disciples for over three years, Jesus told them he was about to leave and that it was to their advantage that he did (John 16:7). I am sure they couldn't imagine how things could get better than daily life with the Son of God, but he promised there was something better to come. Jesus said the Holy Spirit would come actually live in them (John 14:17). Yes, we heard Jesus right. God is going to live *in* you by the Holy Spirit.

There are many things that Jesus could not even communicate with His disciples until the Holy Spirit took up residence inside of them. Jesus promised his disciples that when the Holy Spirit came they would be able to hear God like never before. Now, those who follow Jesus have the Holy Spirit dwelling inside them and are able to hear God personally once again.

> I have many more things to say to you, but you cannot bear *them* now. But when he, the Spirit of truth, comes, he will guide you into all the truth; for he will not speak on his own initiative, but whatever he hears, he will speak; and he will disclose to you what is to come. He will glorify me, for he will take of Mine and will disclose *it* to you. All things that the

Father has are Mine; therefore I said that he takes of Mine and will disclose *it* to you. (John 16:12-15)

Since Jesus was leaving earth, the disciples and subsequent followers of Jesus would need God's assistance in knowing and following his ways. The Holy Spirit has many roles and responsibilities in our lives, but I like how the above passage references him as our "guide." What a practical picture of the kind of communication we receive from the Holy Spirit. A guide is someone who accompanies you in travel to help you reach your destination safely. A guide not only knows where the destination is, but they are familiar with the journey to get there. The Holy Spirit knows where

The Holy Spirit knows where we need to go and he is committed to guiding us each and every day so we can get there.

we need to go and he is committed to guiding us each and every day so we can get there. Therefore, our lives are all about following the leadership of the Holy Spirit.

In Acts chapter 2, the Holy Spirit is poured out on all who believe upon Jesus and as a result, the church begins to experience incredible things including the distribution of God's voice among them individually. Now, everyone can hear from God. We read about angels speaking to people (Acts 8:26), others having visions (Acts 10:9-17), and some even hearing the audible voice of God (Acts 9:3-6). There are numerous accounts of the Holy Spirit communicating to and through Christians in the book of Acts.

It's amazing to me how so many believe that God lives in them by the Holy Spirit, but for some reason he doesn't try to communicate with us as he did in the book of Acts. My belief is that God lives too close to me to say nothing. The Holy Spirit has been speaking to people throughout the last 1,900 years of history and is communicating to all who will listen today. Everyone can hear God, but not everyone does. What we believe about God's voice either empowers or hinders our hearing.

Historical Accounts of Hearing God

These are just a few historical accounts of people who heard God in their day and responded to what He said. The following examples are well documented and have produced fruit in relation to the specific instances of hearing from God. Interestingly, the more I have studied church history, the more accounts of hearing God's voice I have found, so I encourage you to do the same as you build your faith for hearing God.

Polycarp (Bishop of Smyrna) 69 - 155 AD

Polycarp was a man born toward the end of the life of the twelve disciples of Jesus. Scholars believe that he was discipled and appointed as a bishop in Smyrna by the Apostle John himself. Most church historical accounts acknowledge Polycarp to be one of the three apostolic fathers in his day. He is widely known today because of his martyrdom, the account of which can be read in *Foxe's Book of Martyrs*, and in other less well-known literature. Also, Polycarp wrote several epistles, but only one has survived which is called "the epistle sent to the Philippians" in connection with Ignatius.[7] Additionally, there are a few historical documents that record the life of and unique martyrdom of Polycarp where God spoke to him through a vision.

Polycarp was being pursued by hostiles because of his faith in Christ and position in the church, but he was at peace in his heart and did not fear what may come. One night, during a normal time of prayer, Polycarp received a vision from God. In this vision he could see a pillow under his head that seemed to be on fire. As he came out of this vision he turned to those who were with him and said to them prophetically, "I must be burnt alive."[8]

Three days after receiving this vision from the Lord, Polycarp was betrayed into the hands of his pursuers. While in custody he was told he must revile and renounce the name of Christ, which he refused to do. His vision from the Lord came true. Polycarp was sentenced to die by being burned alive at the stake. God prepared this incredible man for his death by speaking to him through a vision. This was not the only recorded time that we read about God speaking to Polycarp, but it is the most well known.

St. Augustine (Bishop of Hippo) 354 - 430 AD

St. Augustine was an early Christian theologian and bishop within the Catholic Church. He was and is widely known and recognized for his recorded sermons and books which are still in print and read all over the world today. There are several recorded instances in which Augustine writes about hearing the voice of God, but the one that is most well known surrounds the time of his conversion.

According to his own account,[9] Augustine was sitting with a friend one day and heard an audible voice that sounded much like a child's. The voice said to him repeatedly, "Take up and read." When he heard the voice he believed it to be a divine exhortation to open the Bible and read whatever passage he happened to turn to. It just so happened that Augustine turned to this passage in Romans:

> Let us behave properly as in the day, not in carousing and
> drunkenness, not in sexual promiscuity and sensuality, not in
> strife and jealousy. But put on the Lord Jesus Christ, and make
> no provision for the flesh in regard to *its* lusts. (Rom. 13:13-14)

It was because of this experience, among other influences, that Augustine decided to convert to Christianity. Sometime after this experience he was baptized and began studying for the priesthood. In 391 AD, Augustine was ordained as a priest and continued in his writings which have greatly influenced western Christianity and philosophy to this day. Here is a man deeply imbedded in the history of Christianity who heard God's voice and was changed because of it.

Aimee Semple McPherson (Evangelist) October 1890 - September 1944

Aimee Semple McPherson is arguably the greatest and most well-known Christian woman leader in the church's history. Aimee was born during the Pentecostal reformation wherein she became a key leader for the furtherance of the gospel of Jesus Christ through the Pentecostal expression. Many books and articles have been written to chronicle her incredible yet controversial life.[10]

Countless stories could be told of how Aimee heard the voice of God and obeyed with great urgency. While many might refute aspects of these stories, the fruit of her ministry bears witness to the activity of the Holy Spirit. Early on in her ministry Aimee wrestled in her heart with her call to preach the gospel, but one day, in the midst of great sickness and a major medical operation, Aimee heard the voice of the Lord say repeatedly, "*Now will you go?*" to which she finally replied "Yes, Lord—I'll go."[11]

Aimee Semple McPherson preached to millions through tent revivals, radio, and churches all over. Her commitment to the gospel and the local church led her to found Angelus Temple (the church she pastored in Los Angeles, CA), and ultimately the Foursquare Denomination, which is still flourishing today. Her exploits were numerous, her influence was incredible, and it all started from her response to God's question to her, "*Will you go?*" I pray that we would hear God and respond to him as Aimee Semple McPherson did.

Modern Accounts of Hearing God

These are some recent accounts of people who heard God and responded to Him. All of these stories are written by people that I know personally and fully trust, so as you read please extend the same trust toward them and be encouraged by what God has done.

Roberta (Mother)

One morning as I was going about my morning chores, I heard the Lord say, "Pray for Lindsey, regarding suicide." Although I did not hear

God's voice audibly, this statement was so clear that it might as well have been. I knew that he was referring to my niece and I was shaken to the core. I immediately began to pray and ask what else I was to do. That afternoon I called my daughter who was very close to Lindsey, thinking that she might know if Lindsey was struggling with depression. She was not aware of anything so I called my sister, who told me Lindsey was home for a visit and seemed fine; in fact, she seemed more connected to the family than she had been for quite some time.

Several weeks later I received a phone call from my sister saying that Lindsey was in the hospital from an overdose, an attempt at suicide. This began a season of intense prayer and walking alongside my sister's family. That year, I was studying the book of Daniel and felt like every time Daniel was on his face praying, I was doing the same. At one point, I felt the Lord ask me to call the entire family and ask them to take a day of fasting and prayer for Lindsey. It was at this point I discovered that the spirit of depression and suicide was in our family line, and the battle in prayer became a battle for my entire family.

Eight months later, after at least two more suicide attempts, Lindsey entered the Teen Challenge program in California. I was called to walk alongside her by volunteering at a Teen Challenge center here in Washington. As I walked alongside Lindsey I had the honor of ministering to her from time to time, one time sharing a dream God had given me that she was in. In the dream, Lindsey asked a question. It was the same question that she had written in her journal months before. God used the dream to reveal His great love for her.

Three-and-a-half years later, I heard the Lord sweetly say, "I am releasing you from prayer for Lindsey and her soon-to-be husband will now cover her in prayer." As of this writing, they are celebrating their second anniversary and expecting their first child, a son.

Marcia (Pastor)

I had been attending a college about four hours from my home-town and one weekend I needed to drive home for a family event. I decided to make the drive Friday night but when the time came I was totally exhausted and felt it would be too far for me to drive that night by myself. Knowing that I would go early Saturday morning, I spent the evening with my friends and ended up getting very little sleep to prepare me for the drive. With two hours of sleep, I got up for my trip home even more exhausted than I was the night before. An hour into my drive I could barely stay awake or keep my eyes open so I pulled over to take a nap in my car. I entered a deserted strip mall parking lot to take a quick nap and parked in the middle of the lot just to stay safe. It was about 4:30 a.m. so the parking lot was completely empty. I took my keys out of the ignition, double-checked that all my doors were locked, and laid down to fall asleep.

After sleeping for about 15 minutes I heard a voice tell me, "Wake up, put your keys in your ignition, and drive." Without thinking about it, I did the exact thing that I heard to do. In the process of doing this I glanced out the passenger side window and saw a man standing right outside my car with his hands on my window. I smiled and waved at the man as I drove away. When the man saw me he was completely startled and quickly stepped away from my car. For some time I thought nothing of this encounter as I got on the freeway and finished my drive completely awake.

A couple of miles down the road, I begin to think about what had just happened. It dawned on me that the man in the parking lot was trying to get into my car while I was sleeping. The more I thought about this, the more I knew I had truly heard the voice of God in that moment. By listening to the voice of God I was protected from whatever the man had intended for me. I spent the rest of the drive praising and worshiping God, thanking Him for His mercy and protection over my life.

Chuck (Pastor)

When I turned 18 years old I found myself depressed and hopeless, believing that life was hard and only going to get harder. Instead of being challenged to do great things with my life I was tired and exhausted with the challenges I had faced. In order to end my hardship, I made plans to kill myself. I was raised in the mountains near a lake and had spent many summers swimming there. This was a lake that I knew well and had even almost unintentionally drowned in a few times. Having these brushes with death caused me to think that drowning myself would somehow be the best way.

One morning I got up and drove to that same mountain lake. It was December and the early morning frost still covered the ground. I thought that if I could swim to the middle of the lake the cold mountain water would do the job in ending my life. When I put my feet into the water they went numb instantly and it occurred to me that the desperate plan I had made would probably work. As I was getting ready to jump in I heard an audible voice say to me, "Why don't you give me a try?" The voice was loud and clear and even sounded like it came from someone standing right behind me. I turned and found no one, so I called out, "Hello, is anybody there?" I could see for quite a distance around me but nobody was there, so I just stood there confused, wondering who had just spoken to me.

In that moment it dawned on me that what I heard was the voice of God. Instead of being happy or excited I was angry. "Why would God wait until my feet are in the water and I am about to take the dive before saying anything to me?" I thought. I was so angry I began to yell into the air. "God, if that is you, I will make you a deal. I will go wherever you want me to go, talk to whomever you want me to talk to, and do whatever you want me to do. I will even go to church every Sunday, if you will only make me happy."

Before the words left my mouth I felt what I can only describe as peace enter my body. It started in the top of my head and moved through my whole body like a wave. It made me feel warm on that cold day and I had the impression that I could handle any hardship that came my way. After that I went home and tried to find a church that could teach me about the God behind the voice I had heard. Today, as a pastor, I get to help others discover the God who saved me from both physical and spiritual death!

Trevor (Youth Pastor)

My oldest brother serves in the military and, while deployed to Afghanistan, my family and I would pray for him regularly. While I was coming home late one night, the Lord spoke to me about praying for my brother's protection, so I began to pray with a clear urgency from the Lord. Shortly after, I got home and went to bed not fully understanding what had just happened. The next morning I woke up as my dad rushed into my room with news that my brother was hit by an IED (Improvised Explosive Device). From the phone call we received, we knew my brother was in critical condition but we had no specific answers or details surrounding this event. About two hours later my brother called us to let us know he had minor injuries and would be fine.

When my brother came home from his tour in Afghanistan, he told us the full story of all that had happened surrounding this event. Incredibly, the timing of my prayer was directly synched to the timing of this event. There is no doubt that God spoke to me about praying and then answered that prayer by protecting my brother and our family from great loss. I am so grateful that God speaks to us and answers our prayers.

Chapter 2 Review Questions

1. How do the biblical accounts of hearing from God differ from your experiences? If there is a difference, why do you think that is the case?

2. What historical accounts of people who heard from God inspire you? Why?

3. What are the clearest examples of hearing from God in your own experience? What about the accounts of other people you know or have heard about?

4. What encouraged you most about this chapter and how will you apply it to your life?

CHAPTER 3

HEARING GOD AND THE BIBLE

Before I was a Christian I can honestly say that I was scared of the Bible. I remember a handful of times where I sat down and was overwhelmed with conviction as I noticed a Bible sitting right next to me. Part of this unusual reverence was the result of being raised as a Christian and choosing to rebel against what I was taught. I think the other side of my reverence came from the true Author of the Bible—the Holy Spirit. One day I even picked up a Bible as a non-Christian and started reading the book of Revelation. It freaked me out! I must have read several chapters that day because all I could remember was dragons, harlots, eagles, wars, plagues, and the world coming to an end.

When I gave my heart to Jesus I was no longer scared of the Bible; I was excited about reading this holy book. I took the bus to work every day and spent the entire time reading, highlighting, underlining, and falling in love with God's word. Early on in my Christian walk I made a commitment to read the Bible every day. By God's grace, I have kept that commitment. I have a God-given reverence for the Bible that effects my life on a daily basis in everything I think, see, and do.

Friends, the Bible is more than a book. The Bible is more than letters on a page containing good thoughts, historical accounts, great poetry, and a general outline of God's plan. The Bible is God's word. We should take seriously the way we view and approach the Bible because how we perceive God's word will determine our overall spiritual health.

Maybe you were aware of the basic facts about the Bible, that it is a collection of 66 books, written by over forty authors, involving three different languages, and spans a time period of 1,500 years. Maybe you know that the Bible contains multiple accounts of history, hundreds of fulfilled and yet-to-be-fulfilled prophecies, ancient proverbs and poetry, and important first-century letters. It's possible that you learned how the Bible contains a unity of subject, structure, and spirit with a consistency of doctrinal and moral teachings throughout its entirety. But do these facts alone bring you to your knees before the God who not only brought this book into existence, but also makes it alive to those who walk with Him? Do we treat the Bible as God's *holy* word, or as just another *set* of words, like we do with so many other books, teachings, movies, scholarly and historical accounts?

It seems that everywhere I go to teach and minister there are a handful of people who need to know where I stand on the Bible. I really appreciate those who need me to state, for the record, my overall stance and commitment to the Bible as I discuss a topic like hearing from God. My view of scripture is very fundamental but I don't personally think the purpose of the Bible and the hearing of God's voice are given for the same reason.

I don't believe that you can truly understand what God is saying by his Spirit unless you understand what he has said through his word.

Some people, no matter what I say, will think that I have a low view of the Bible because I believe God still speaks today. This couldn't be farther from the truth.

My view of scripture, and my commitment to live out and experience scripture is what leads me to the conclusions that you will read about in this book. When we hear from God, we are not seeking to rewrite the Bible, add to the Bible, or take away from the Bible. When we hear from God personally we are experiencing the reality of the Bible in our current context. Hearing God's voice and reading, studying, and applying the Bible are not the same things and they are not given for the same purposes.

The Bible Is God's Voice

I don't believe that you can truly understand what God is saying by his Spirit unless you understand what he has said through his word. Why is that? Because the Bible is more than God's voice to the original readers. In its uniqueness the Bible remains as the voice of God for us today. The Bible itself claims its origin from God and not merely man.

> *So* we have the prophetic word *made* more sure, to which you do well to pay attention as to a lamp shining in a dark place, until the day dawns and the morning star arises in your hearts. But know this first of all, that no prophecy of Scripture is *a matter* of one's own interpretation, for no prophecy was ever made by an act of human will, but men moved by the Holy Spirit spoke from God. (2 Pet. 1:19-21)

In his letter to some established churches, the Apostle Peter reminds the believing community of many wonderful truths that are extremely important for their lives. At the same time, Peter shares his deep concern regarding the spread of false prophets and destructive teachings that have begun to affect the churches in very serious ways.

Being a direct disciple of Jesus, Peter was an eyewitness of his coming glory (Matt. 17:1-13) and the power of his resurrection (Luke 24:50-53). Peter was able to affirm the fulfillment of prophecies written in the Old Testament as one who literally saw it happen before his eyes. In the above passage Peter mentions that *no* prophecy (Old

Testament scripture) was produced merely by men. The Holy Spirit "moved" upon the writers of scripture, similar to a wind that carries a ship along the water.

While false prophets and heretical teachings were making an appearance in the early church, Peter directed the churches to "pay attention" to the dependable voice of God in scripture. This passage is one of many that reveal the *inspiration* of the Bible. The Bible was inspired by God in that the Holy Spirit spoke these words to those who wrote them down. Peter referred to the Old Testament because it was the only scriptures that they had.

The apostle Paul said something similar to Peter in his letter to Timothy.

> All Scripture is inspired by God and profitable for teaching, for reproof, for correction, for training in righteousness; so that the man of God may be adequate, equipped for every good work. (2 Tim. 3:16-17)

The term "inspired by God" literally means, "God-breathed."[12] Think about that for a moment. All scripture is God-breathed—not some but *all.* In other words, what we have sitting on our shelves or downloaded onto our computers is the voice of God. It contains what God wants us to have and what He wants us to know.

The Bible is infallible which means that it's without error in its original writings. God's Spirit was careful to bring about necessary prophecies and teachings because these words were meant to be the eternal words of God (1 Pet. 1:25). The Bible is the foundation of knowing and hearing God's voice for all people in every generation.

I have mentioned scriptures that point to the Old Testament as being the word (voice) of God, but what about the New Testament? Is the New Testament also on the same level as the Old? The answer to that is simply *yes.* The New Testament writers knew that they were writing scripture. We see this clearly in many of the letters that the apostle Paul wrote and distributed to various churches. For example, look at what Paul writes to the Corinthian church. "But to the married I give instructions, not I, *but the Lord*, that the wife should not leave her husband" (1 Cor. 7:10). Obviously the context is important, but for our conversation, notice how Paul clearly says "not I, but *the Lord*" as he communicates to the church. He makes it clear that this is God's voice and not his own. In Paul's letter to the church at Thessalonica he shares even stronger language to this effect: "For you know what commandments we gave you by *the authority of* the Lord Jesus" (1 Thess. 4:2). Paul and other apostles spoke and wrote commands to the first century believers that they knew were straight from God. After Paul reminds the Thessalonian church of these commands, look at what he says to those who reject his (God's) words: "So, he who rejects *this* is not rejecting man *but the God* who gives His Holy Spirit to you" (1 Thess. 4:8).

When God spoke to the writers of scripture he made sure that there was one hundred percent clarity in their receiving of revelation and one hundred percent accuracy in their writing of his revelation. For scripture to be written as the eternal word (voice) of God there could be no misunderstanding or wrong interpretations involved. This is not to suggest that God doesn't care about the clarity in which we hear him today, but rather I want to emphasize the sovereignty of God over the process of forming scripture. God did not allow the Bible to be wrong and therefore it is in a category of hearing from God all on its own. It's unique and my desire is that everyone would honor it as such.

When we seek to hear God's voice today personally we need to be clear about something—we are not seeking to write or rewrite the Bible. The Bible has been written and its purpose is for all people to have a clear standard concerning that which God wanted us to know. It does not and will not change throughout all generations. The Bible contains unchanging truths like who God is, the fall of man, the plan of salvation through Jesus Christ, and Christ's second coming. The purpose of the Bible is to provide an unchanging foundation for everyone by setting a standard by which everything we hear God say outside of it can be measured.

God has established his voice through his word, the Bible, and he speaks specifically to people within their own contexts and generations through the voice of His Spirit. While we do need to understand it in its context, the Bible is God's voice to us by which we must derive our knowledge of God and his plan. We need the Bible. Like David,

> **God has established his voice through his word, the Bible, and he speaks specifically to people within their own contexts and generations through the voice of His Spirit.**

may we remember that God's word shows us where we are and where we are going and that, without it, we are lost.

> "Your word is a lamp to my feet And a light to my path."
> (Ps. 119:105)

The Harmony of God's Voice

From early on I became familiar with many theological differences in Christianity including those related to hearing God's voice. During the first week of being a Christian I was launched into the reality of God's voice without any understanding whatsoever. I had literal dreams, strong impressions, and other interesting experiences that I didn't know what to do with. I shared these experiences with the leaders at the church I was attending and they pretty much told me to ignore those things and read the Bible. Not only was I already reading the Bible but I had also started having some of the same experiences that I was reading about, which encouraged me all the more. My excitement caused me to share these experiences with others which didn't always seem to go well.

I had a few people sit down with me and explain how the things that were happening to me no longer happened today. Can you imagine that conversation? Yeah, it pretty much went how you might imagine. Needless to say I was really confused. The people that shared these things with me were well-meaning Christians who loved Jesus and the Bible. They didn't use the Bible much, other than one misquoted verse here and there, to inform my experience and perspective on the issue of hearing from God. I thought it was odd that people who loved the Bible so much didn't use the Bible to articulate such a strong position on what God does and doesn't do today. While they were trying to ensure that I didn't develop my theology based on my experiences, I was wondering why they developed their theology from a lack of experience.

There are people who believe that God no longer speaks except through the Bible. While I can appreciate their jealousy for the word, that kind of thinking is just simply not true. There are also people who disregard the Bible or treat it with very little reverence. They honor what they believe the Holy Spirit is telling them but don't realize that the Bible is the primary way we discern God's voice, namely the things they think God is telling them. This can be extremely dangerous which could lead to error, deception, or worse.

The Bible is like a house. The Old Testament is the foundation and the New Testament is the house which is built upon the foundation. When we hear God's voice through the Holy Spirit it's not an addition to the house or another house entirely but rather it is something that fits in the house like furniture, paintings to put on the wall, or maybe a special light fixture. In the same way, hearing from God must work in harmony with the Bible; because whatever God says today will be congruent with what He has already said in the Bible.

The life of the Apostle Paul demonstrates the harmony of God's voice in such a unique way. Paul knew the Old Testament scriptures very well and he also knew the words of Jesus through the influence of the other apostles and his own personal encounters with Jesus (Acts 9). When Paul traveled on his missionary journeys, the Holy Spirit would regularly speak to him about what to do and where to go. A story that illustrates this well is found in Acts chapter 16.

> They passed through the Phrygian and Galatian region, having been forbidden by the Holy Spirit to speak the word in Asia; and after they came to Mysia, they were trying to go into Bithynia, and the Spirit of Jesus did not permit them; and passing by Mysia, they came down to Troas. A vision appeared to Paul in the night: a man of Macedonia was standing and appealing to him, and saying, "Come over to Macedonia and help us." When he had seen the vision, immediately we sought to go into Macedonia, concluding that God had called us to preach the gospel to them. So putting out to sea from Troas, we ran a straight course to Samothrace, and on the day following to Neapolis; and from there to Philippi, which is a leading city of the district of Macedonia, a *Roman* colony; and we were staying in this city for some days. And on the Sabbath day we went outside the gate to a riverside, where we were supposing that there would be a place of prayer; and we sat down and began speaking to the women who had assembled. (Acts 16:6-13)

Paul and his companions were traveling missionaries who were spreading the gospel of Jesus Christ and making disciples from city to city. Paul didn't need a prophetic word to do what he was doing in spreading the word because he knew the general plan and will of God from what Jesus taught about preaching the gospel and making disciples (Matt. 28:18-20). While Paul was trying to enter Bithynia, he mentions that "the Spirit of Jesus did not permit them" (Acts 16:7).

If Paul had only the Bible as his means of knowing what God was saying to him, how would he know not to enter a certain region? He wouldn't! That's why the Holy Spirit spoke to him about what to do in that situation. Apply this scenario to your own life. The Bible says to preach the gospel to every creation and make disciples of all nations (Mark 16:15; Matt. 28:19). How would we know to remain in one area or move onto another if we only had the Bible as God's voice?

In addition to these thoughts, consider what Paul told the Thessalonian church regarding the resistance in coming to see them.

> But we, brethren, having been taken away from you for a short while—in person, not in spirit—were all the more eager with great desire to see your face. For we wanted to come to you—I, Paul, more than once—and *yet* Satan hindered us. (1 Thess. 2:17-18)

Satan hindered Paul from entering the city of Thessalonica. In our previous verse we read how the Holy Spirit did not permit Paul to enter Bithynia (Acts 16). If Paul believed that God only spoke through the Bible then how would he know where to go or who was even hindering him from entering a city? If he didn't believe that God would speak by his Spirit would Paul have assumed that the resistance to enter Bithynia was Satan? Seriously though, how would he know?

I realize that Paul had a special calling in being an apostle and planting the gospel in the first century, but why would we think it is any different for us today? You can't just say, "We have the completed Bible and they didn't!" The problem of knowing where to go still exists no matter how many Bibles we have. Yes, the Bible tells us what to do, but the Spirit tells us where to go and how to *apply* what we are doing in our specific context.

The harmony of God's voice—coming both through the Bible and through his Spirit—is beautiful and it grieves me that so many confuse this issue. Throughout Scripture we can clearly see how the people of God understood the importance of the Bible and the present voice of God and I contend that we need the same perspective today.

Imagine a philharmonic orchestra with sixty-six instruments playing a classic song with such beauty and perfection that it seems like it couldn't get any better. Then, for the next song, they bring out twenty more people with four additional instruments. The only reason they would bring out more instruments is to enhance the song through other sounds that work in harmony with what they already have.

Could you imagine one of those instruments playing a different song or way out of tune? How fast would that musician get dismissed from the orchestra? Let's just say that might be the end of a career for said orchestra musician. Without harmony the additional instruments ruin the entire song and make the orchestra sound terrible. As people who hear from God, we must ensure that what we hear harmonizes with what God has already said in scripture. When we do that, our lives are a beautiful sound to God and to those surrounding us.

The Same Author

Have you ever been told, "If you want to hear God's voice just open the Bible and He will speak to you?" I have heard this statement quite a bit and before I spent significant time in the Bible I had no problem agreeing with it. Now, I see things differently from the idea that statement conveys. As you know, I believe that the Bible is God's eternal word. I heartily say "Amen!" to this reality. However, does knowing the purpose and place of the Bible equate to hearing God's voice every time we read it? Before you say yes, let's think about this for a moment.

On a particular sabbath day, Jesus went to Jerusalem for one of the feasts. When he arrived, he passed by a small pool where many sick people had gathered. Jesus had a specific encounter with a man who had been sick for thirty-eight years, but through the power of God Jesus healed the man of his illness. This healing caused an uproar among the Jewish leaders, supposedly because Jesus healed this man on the Sabbath, which was forbidden through their interpretation of the Law (Old Testament). For the next while Jesus engaged in some aggressive debates with the religious leaders where he ultimately calls into question their relationship with God and their *true* knowledge of the scriptures.

> And the Father who sent Me, He has testified of Me. You have neither heard His voice at any time nor seen His form. You do not have His word abiding in you, for you do not believe Him whom He sent. (John 5:37-38)

As we read this passage we need to understand that the people Jesus rebukes are considered to be scholars of the Bible. Note that he addresses them with, "you have neither heard His voice" (John 5:37) and, "you do not have His word abiding in you" (John 5:38). But they know the Bible, right? Is it possible to read and memorize the Bible and still not hear God? Absolutely! Why? When you read words and interpret their meaning apart from the author you will end up with an incorrect understanding. Clearly, Jesus wasn't addressing whether or not they had read the Bible; he was addressing whether or not the Author of the Bible was present in their understanding, which makes the difference. Jesus goes on to say:

> You search the Scriptures because you think that in them you have eternal life; it is these that testify about Me; and you are unwilling to come to Me so that you may have life. (John 5:39-40)

The purpose of the Bible is to lead us to the Author—God. These men who spent the majority of their lives studying the scriptures had missed something huge: their connection to the author. The Holy Spirit not only caused the scriptures to be penned, but he also is the one who causes them to be understood. Without God giving us revelation about what the Bible means, all of our studying, interpretations, and opinions about the Bible are worthless.

67

of our studying, interpretations, and opinions about the Bible are worthless. Let me say it again—worthless!

The Bible is more than a textbook to be studied in a classroom. It contains spiritual words of life that have spiritual power because they are born of the Holy Spirit. While on earth, Jesus regularly said things to people that they didn't understand. Why? He explains why when he says, "It is the Spirit who gives life; the flesh profits nothing; the words that I have spoken to you are spirit and are life" (John 6:63). Understanding and obeying what Jesus said and what the whole Bible teaches is not possible without God's gift of revelation to us. In other words, reading the Bible is not enough; you also need God to communicate to you as you read the Bible. If the Bible is to carry any real weight in the way we live our lives, we also need God to communicate to us personally about what we read.

As a person who studies the Bible every day I have read some verses hundreds of times before I actually understood them. Is that because I somehow got smarter over the years or was it that one day the Holy Spirit illuminated a passage and brought revelation to my heart? What I am trying to say is that the whole issue of hearing God speak is connected directly to reading the Bible. The same one who wrote the Bible and reveals the meaning of the Bible is the same one who speaks into my heart concerning how, when, and where to apply the Bible. It is not enough to simply hear God speak apart from the Bible, but neither is it enough to simply read the Bible without hearing God speak to my heart words of revelation and direction. Successfully hearing God speak to us requires that we learn to harmonize the reading of his word with the hearing of his voice.

Chapter 3 Review Questions

1. What is the difference between reading scripture and hearing God's voice personally? Which voice has more authority and why?

2. How does the combination of knowing the Bible and hearing God's voice help you know what God is saying? Can you provide any clear examples?

3. Have you ever been taught that God only speaks through the Bible? Do you feel like that is a biblical idea? Why or why not?

4. Why is it important to know the different purposes for the Bible and hearing God personally?

5. What encouraged you most about this chapter and how will you apply it to your life?

PART II

GOD'S VOICE: UNDERSTANDING WHAT IT IS AND WHAT IT'S NOT

CHAPTER 4
UNDERSTANDING HOW GOD SPEAKS

One of the more common things I hear people say is, "I don't hear God's voice!" As you can already tell, I don't believe that is actually the case, but I do think it's a symptom of something much bigger that we need to explore. I believe God speaks to everyone, but that doesn't mean everyone will discern when or *how* God is trying to communicate with them. What we really mean when we say "I don't hear God" is probably better stated, "I don't hear God clearly," or, "God doesn't speak to me the way that others claim to hear Him." Therefore, knowing *how* God communicates to people is essential to hearing Him and not missing what might be right in front of us. In the Bible, God spoke to people in very different ways, some of which may even seem odd to us. I often wish that God spoke to me clearly, but that just hasn't been my experience. What about you? Have you ever longed for clarity regarding the voice of God in your life? Wouldn't it be great if we could dial up 1-800-HEAVEN, ask our questions, and receive a clear answer within moments? I think that would be awesome! Not only is that not the case, but it's not supposed to be that way.

The very first week of becoming a Christian, I remember having vivid, detailed dreams that seemed incredibly real as I woke up. After the third dream I knew something was going on that couldn't be a figment of my imagination or some bad pizza I had eaten the night before. I began talking about these dreams to other Christians who essentially didn't know what to tell me other than, "well, just keep reading the Bible." So I did. I read the Bible as much as I could. But guess what I found the more I read the Bible? I found that God spoke to people in very different ways, including through dreams. The combination of studying scripture and personal experience have helped me understand that God's voice is not always an actual, audible voice. If I were to say "God spoke to me" to someone, unless they knew the principles I am sharing in this book (or books like it), they probably would think that God spoke audibly, and specifically in my own language. However, this may be the furthest thing from what actually happened in my hearing the voice of God. This is why we need to not only understand the different ways God communicates, but learn to share with others *how* God speaks to us, which will help them as they learn to hear God for themselves.

We live in a world in which people use multiple forms of communication regularly. I was at the bank the other day and pulled up to the drive-through ATM to make a deposit with my debit card. As I was going through my transaction I noticed there were Braille characters below each number on the ATM. Now I have no idea why they would have Braille on a drive-through ATM machine, but this exemplifies a form of communication that goes under our noses everyday. Several people at our church are fluent in sign language and able to communicate with those who cannot speak using a verbal language. Also, just today I used my phone to send text messages and my computer to type emails that were sent into cyberspace or airwaves, somehow reaching my intended destination as clearly as I sent them. These are just a few of the many ways we communicate with each other daily, making it easier to understand that God has chosen to use multiple forms of communication to get our attention, teach us something, provide direction, or just tell us how much he loves us. The point is that God doesn't always use his audible voice or our native language when speaking to us.

As we look at the different ways that God speaks to us, I want you to know that these are by no means the only ways, but I have found these to be more common both in my experience and in scripture. While many of the scriptures I refer to do not specifically say, "This is how God will speak to you," they do represent specific interactions that God had with others which should prove helpful for us if and when God speaks to us the same way.

The Bible

As you know, I have devoted a whole chapter of this book to the role of the Bible in hearing from God, so I won't repeat the things we have already discussed. But as we move through the various forms of communication I need to say with extreme clarity that I will always contend that *the* primary way we hear and discern God's voice begins and ends with the Bible. I believe the Bible is true, every word of it. The Bible is infallible and contains the general, unchanging will of God for every believer of every generation. Consider this truth as you seek to hear God better in your life. The Bible is always the first place we go to hear God and it is the first place we go to discern what we believe the Holy Spirit might be saying to us personally. With this in mind, I encourage you to consider how you prioritize the Bible in your daily life; it truly does make the difference.

The Bible is always the first place we go to hear God and it is the first place we go to discern what we believe the Holy Spirit might be saying to us personally.

The apostle Paul wrote two letters to his son in the faith, Timothy. The truths contained in his second letter, written toward the end of his life, are in many ways the final things Paul wanted to say, making them extremely important. Paul wanted Timothy to understand that the Bible is "inspired" or more literally "God-breathed," and that the books contained therein have true power to transform lives. The Apostle Peter also wrote with the same notion to his readers that the scripture is not of human will, but is "inspired" by God's Spirit.

> All Scripture is *inspired* by God and profitable for teaching, for reproof, for correction, for training in righteousness; so that the man of God may be adequate, equipped for every good work. (2 Tim. 3:16-17)

> But know this first of all, that no prophecy of Scripture is *a matter* of one's own interpretation, for no prophecy was ever made by an act of human will, but men *moved by the Holy Spirit spoke from God.* (2 Pet. 1:20-21)

As the Bible is the primary voice of God in our lives, it's helpful to know how God will speak to us through it. Generally, there are two ways that you will hear God speak as it relates to the Bible. The first is that God will speak to you through the Bible as you *study* it. Have you ever experienced a moment where a verse jumped off the page and spoke to you in a deeply personal way? I sure have. Although this doesn't happen to me every time I read the Bible, I sure look forward to the times that it does happen. Just recently I was reading the book of James and this very thing happened to me. It says in James 1:5, "But if any of you lacks wisdom, let him ask of God, who gives to all generously and without reproach, and it will be given to him." The word "generously" jumped off the page and caused me to think rather deeply about how generous God really is. If my view of God informs my interaction with Him, then how important is it for me to see him as a generous Father? I personally read the Bible every day and as I do I write in a journal the various things that

I believe God is speaking to me. If we want to hear from God, we must read the Bible regularly. It must be a priority.

If my view of God informs my interaction with Him, then how important is it for me to see him as a generous Father?

The second way that God will use the Bible to speak to us is by *reminding us of different verses* in our daily lives or specific circumstances. I can remember early on in my Christian life that I would regularly share my testimony with people at the coffee shop down the street from where I lived. One evening I was getting coffee and I encountered an old friend who wasn't aware of my recent transformation in Christ. I shared with her my testimony and she began asking me a billion questions which I didn't have many good answers for. She had great questions, but I didn't know the Bible well enough and my experience with God was pretty much contained in my testimony and didn't seem enough to convince her to believe. We walked outside still engaged in conversation, and as I listened to her my mind started looming with Bible verses that I had just read that week. It was like the Holy Spirit made several chapters from the book of John accessible to me in that moment so that I could answer many of the questions she was asking. This was a true supernatural occurrence. Although this woman didn't become a Christian that night, she did give her life to Jesus just a few months later.

The moments before Jesus' betrayal, he shared many important things with his disciples. Instead of expecting them to remember it all he let them know that the Holy Spirit would remind them of what He was saying.

> These things I have spoken to you while abiding with you. But the Helper, the Holy Spirit, whom the Father will send in My name, He will teach you all things, and *bring to your remembrance all that I said to you.* (John 14:25-26)

The Holy Spirit takes what we have read (and sometimes have not read) in the Bible and reminds us in the moments when we truly need it. If we are going to understand what God *is* saying by his Spirit, then we first need to understand what God *has* said in the Bible.

Impressions

An impression is an internal sense in which you feel, think, or know something regarding a person or a situation. A technical, basic definition of the word impression can refer to an indent or mark produced by outside pressure. I think this natural definition can help us understand how impressions work when God is speaking to us this way. A good illustration of

> **If we are going to understand what God *is* saying by his Spirit, then we first need to understand what God *has* said in the Bible.**

this could be a footprint in the snow. Do you remember being outside in a snow storm and seeing your foot print with each step? If you're outside long enough, you will notice that your footprint gets covered back up with snow within minutes. That is what impressions can be like. God's Spirit will impress something on the inside of you that he wants you to act on, pray about, or share with someone else for their benefit. In my experience, if you don't do something with that impression initially, you most likely will forget that it even happened, much like the footprint getting covered back up with snow.

There are no direct references to the word "impression" in the Bible, mainly because this word is meant to describe various experiences that seem common to many. One instance of an impression in the Bible is found in Acts chapter 27. The Apostle Paul had been imprisoned for some time and in the process appealed to stand trial before Caesar. Shortly after making his appeal, Paul was sent to Rome on a boat to stand trial for what he was being accused of. During the voyage their ship began to experience some troubling waters and the Lord gave Paul an impression of what was going to happen.

> When considerable time had passed and the voyage was now dangerous, since even the fast was already over, Paul *began* to admonish them, and said to them, *"Men, I perceive that the voyage will certainly be with damage and great loss, not only of the cargo and the ship, but also of our lives."* But the centurion was more persuaded by the pilot and the captain of the ship than by what was being said by Paul. (Acts 27:9-11)

These impressions can often seem like a gut feeling, which is very easy to overlook. The more we employ what we think God is saying to us, the easier it gets to determine the accuracy of the impressions of the Holy Spirit. It is by acting upon impressions that we begin to understand how they work. Sometimes I get a strong feeling that I need to talk to or call someone that I just saw or was just thinking about. These are the kind of impressions that are most common in my life. Regardless of how or when they come, cultivating our sensitivity to the Holy Spirit will help us pick up on the subtleties of the impressions God gives us.

Our Thoughts

Another important way that God will speak to us is through our thoughts. I find this to be extremely common for me and many others. Typically, I will be driving down the road and a thought will pop in my mind: "How is John doing?" This will sound a lot like my voice, and at first I normally think it's just a random thought about a person I haven't seen for a while. If I decide to call John, more times than not, my phone call was timely and extremely encouraging as we talk and pray about something he is going through.

God cares about everything in our lives, even the little stuff. I can't tell you how many times I have lost or misplaced my keys, important tool or phone and begin to pray franticly as I tear the house apart. Not long after praying, "God, please show me where my keys are," guess what happens? That's right! A thought pops into my mind which reveals the last place I put my keys or missing item. God speaks into our thoughts a lot more than we may realize and as we learn to ask Him for these thoughts and reminders He will give them in very practical ways.

The Bible has a lot to say about our minds. In 1 Corinthians 2:16, Apostle Paul tells the us that "we have the mind of Christ." In other words, as we are born of the Spirit, we are born to think the way that Jesus does; we should then believe that there will be a consistent flow of God's thoughts streaming through our minds. This doesn't mean that everything we think is from God, but it does mean that God has permanent access to our minds and will speak into our thoughts more regularly than we might realize. This of course leads us to a very important conclusion: not every thought that comes into your mind originates from you. Most of our thoughts are the result of a healthy, properly-functioning brain, while other thoughts are from the Lord and some possibly from the demonic realm. I don't want to give too much credit to the devil since we all still have our own flesh to contend with (Gal. 5:17). However, we will encounter demonic thoughts from time to time and need to be able to discern the difference between those thoughts, our own, and the Lord's. Learning to discern like this will help us as we seek to receive from the Lord in daily life.

There are several scriptures that reference "God's thoughts" within certain contexts. In Psalms, for example, King David speaks of God's thoughts toward us:

> Many, O Lord my God, are the wonders which You have done, *And Your thoughts toward us; There is none to compare with You. If I would declare and speak of them, They would be too numerous to count.* (Ps. 40:5)

As we seek to hear from God, one thing we could ask him, especially while praying for others, is to ask the Lord what *he* thinks of that individual: "Lord, what are your thoughts about this person?" If God has a million amazing thoughts toward each one of us, we should ask him to share his thoughts with us in order to encourage one another. As you welcome and receive God's thoughts both for yourself and for others, your mind will begin to reflect the very mind of Christ.

Visions

We can define a vision as, "spiritual sight given by the Holy Spirit that is meant to reveal God's heart about something or someone, including oneself." The Bible references many visions in both the Old and New Testaments. Visions can be literal, wherein what you see describes something that has happened or will happen (Acts 16:9-10). They can also be symbolic, requiring an interpretation from the Holy Spirit in order to understand the message (Acts 10:9-16).

When I was a young Christian, a friend of mine invited me to attend a mid-week service with him at his church. We arrived at the church building a little late and quietly entered the sanctuary during worship. I had never been to this church before but my friend told me the church was awesome and I would really like the pastor. From the back row of the sanctuary we joined others in singing familiar worship songs. I knew the songs well enough to close my eyes as I worshiped Jesus, but when I opened them something really crazy happened. With my very own eyes I could literally see smoke all over the sanctuary. At the time I did not understand visions, so it did not occur to me that I was having one at that moment. I opened and closed my eyes at least three times to make sure I was really seeing smoke, yet every time I opened my eyes the smoke was still there.

This lasted for about a minute until I finally nudged my friend and said, "Do you see that?" He replied, "See what?" Looking at him while pointing into the thin air I said, "See the smoke!" He looked at me like I was crazy, which only affirmed how I was already feeling, and within a few minutes the experience was over and I was left wondering what had happened.

This was my introduction to God's picture language called *visions*. At the time I had never thought about, read about, or heard a sermon about visions from God. The many questions that followed my experience led me into the scriptures, which had a lot more to say about visions than I had imagined. First, with the coming of the Holy Spirit in the book of Acts, the Apostle Peter quotes Joel:

> "AND IT SHALL BE IN THE LAST DAYS," God says,
> "THAT I WILL POUR FORTH OF MY SPIRIT ON ALL
> MANKIND; AND YOUR SONS AND YOUR DAUGH-
> TERS SHALL PROPHESY, AND YOUR YOUNG MEN
> SHALL SEE VISIONS, AND YOUR OLD MEN SHALL
> DREAM DREAMS; EVEN ON MY BONDSLAVES,
> BOTH MEN AND WOMEN, I WILL IN THOSE DAYS
> POUR FORTH OF MY SPIRIT And they shall prophesy."
> (Acts 2:17-18)

While the concept of having a vision was not new to the people that the Apostle Peter was addressing, they believed that the only people who received the outpouring of the Holy Spirit (thus unique visions and dreams) were prophets, priests and kings, according to the examples within the Old Testament. So, in quoting Joel, Peter was explaining to them that the Spirit is poured out on all kinds of people, which they were witnessing but not understanding at first. Due to this, it would become more normal for the people *themselves* to have the same kinds of visions and dreams from the Lord, inspired by his Spirit. This is truly amazing!

When I saw the smoke fill the sanctuary of my friend's church, there was no literal message in this so I looked into the Bible for similar experiences. In 1 Kings 8, King Solomon was dedicating the temple that Israel had just built for the Lord and suddenly the temple was filled with a cloud in the midst of which the priests could not stand. Additionally, in Isaiah 6, the prophet had a vision of the Lord in his temple, and "the temple filled with smoke" (Isa. 6:4). After looking at several references regarding smoke and even clouds in scripture, I discovered this can simply represent the presence of the Lord. For me, the fact that I encountered the presence of the Lord in such a way at this church indicated somehow that God wanted me to make this church my home, which I did.

The final thing about visions we need to discuss is that there are two ways in which you will typically receive them. The first is internally. Usually during prayer, maybe even with your eyes closed, you will see a collection of pictures or something like a movie clip in your mind. This tends to be the normal way I receive visions, which makes sense when you consider that that Holy Spirit lives within you. The second way you may receive a vision is externally, or more commonly referred to as an *open vision*, which occurs when God opens your physical eyes to see things in the spiritual realm. I had an open vision when I saw the smoke filling the building at my friend's church. A classic example of an open vision is found in 2 Kings 6 when Elisha asks God to open his servant's eyes to see the angelic armies in the spiritual realm. When I receive a vision it tends to impact me in a greater way than when God speaks to me in other ways. Knowing this, I think God gives me visions at times when he really needs me to be certain about something. It's true that a picture speaks a thousand words and I appreciate how visions convey God's mind and heart in such a powerful way.

Dreams

If you were to do a quick search for books about dreams on the internet using a familiar search engine, you would quickly discover the hundreds, if not thousands of books devoted to helping people understand what happens when they are asleep. Most of these books consider neither God nor the Bible when trying to learn about dreams. To be honest, I am not familiar with books that provide varied approaches to understanding dreams, I am not even close to understanding everything about the dream life of a follower of Jesus. My perspective on dreams extends only as far as my own experience combined with what I have found in scripture. Regardless, I do want to mention that most people spend close to one-third of their entire lives in sleep. Think about that for a second. God has designed us, at least in this body, to turn off for one-third of each day so our bodies can rest and become replenished. Through various examples from scripture and experience, God seems determined to use that time to communicate with us.

Dreams are very similar to visions except, obviously, you are asleep instead of awake. Both visions and dreams can be literal or symbolic, meaning interpretation may be required to understand the message given. I meet plenty of people who have regular

Both visions and dreams can be literal or symbolic, meaning interpretation may be required to understand the message given.

dreams, yet struggle to understand if they are from God or if they should just be considered a normal part of the sleep-cycle. I also meet people who never have dreams, so when they do, they take them much more seriously, knowing it may be God. I fall into the second category. When those of us who don't remember our dreams very often wake up with a vivid dream still on our minds, it is easier to consider that God may be speaking.

In my life I have experienced only a handful of significant, God-given dreams. There may have been others, but the ones I am sure of have undoubtedly come from God. In the beginning of 2004 I was a youth leader for a small church in Kirkland, Washington. One night I had a dream that I was sitting in the back of a medium-sized church during an evening service. The worship had just finished and one of the pastors stood up and began to share announcements. When the pastor finished the announcements he started introducing the guest speaker for the evening, and also mentioned the speaker was a new staff member at the church. As he began to describe the speaker I realized he was actually talking about me! I looked down at my lap and there was my Bible with some notes crammed in between the middle pages. In shock as to what was happening, I walked up to the front of the church, put my Bible and notes on the podium, and cleared my throat. As I began to speak, all that I could say was, "God loves you, and he wants you to spend time with him. This is what he wants." After the third time of saying this I sensed the strong presence of the Holy Spirit and people everywhere began to weep and repent out of sincere love for God. It was glorious!

Just a few months after this dream, our church in Kirkland decided to close its doors and disperse into other churches. My wife and I tried to attend other churches, but I could not let go of the dream that I received. After a few months we settled into the church that was in my dream and I pursued a career in real estate to provide for my family. We began serving in the church, but my work required most of my time, so I pretty much forgot about the dream entirely. Approximately seven years later, the senior pastor began asking me if I would consider a pastoral position at the church. Initially, I was hesitant because I enjoyed my job and had even started a discipleship ministry on the side, *Ignite Global Ministries*. However, after praying with my wife and considering the dream I was given, I accepted the position and have been enjoying the journey ever since. The awesome

First, dreams can often be *directional*, wherein God will show you where He wants you to go or what He may want you to do.

thing about the fulfillment of this dream is that, at the right time, I understood what the Lord was trying to tell me. He was sharing with me that I was called to encourage the church into a closer walk with Jesus, and I think that has pretty much been true of my ministry.

There are a few key themes in scripture that will help us when God speaks to us through dreams. First, dreams can often be *directional,* wherein God will show you where He wants you to go or what He may want you to do. Directional dreams characterize most of the dreams I receive from God. Shortly after Jesus was born, God gave Joseph a dream to tell him where to go so that Jesus would be protected from King Herod.

> Now when they had gone, behold, an angel of the Lord appeared to Joseph in a dream and said, "Get up! Take the Child and His mother and flee to Egypt, and remain there until I tell you; for Herod is going to search for the Child to destroy Him." So Joseph got up and took the Child and His mother while it was still night, and left for Egypt. He remained there until the death of Herod. *This was* to fulfill what had been spoken by the Lord through the prophet: "OUT OF EGYPT I CALLED MY SON." (Matt. 2:13-15)

This was not the first time that God had spoken to Joseph in a dream, so it may be worth noting that God may establish a pattern of directional dreams if and when He chooses to speak to you this way.

Secondly, dreams in scripture are sometimes *correctional.* A correctional dream is meant to prevent you from continuing in a certain direction or sin that is harming you, your relationship with God, and possibly others around you. In Job we find an interesting insight into correctional dreams.

> Indeed God speaks once, Or twice, *yet* no one notices it. In a dream, a vision of the night, When sound sleep falls on men, While they slumber in their beds, Then He opens the ears of men, And seals their instruction, That He may turn man aside

from his conduct, And keep man from pride; He keeps back
his soul from the pit, And his life from passing over into Sheol.
(Job 33:14-18)

This passage reveals how God may use dreams to impart instruction, turn us from our current choices, and keep us from pride in order to rescue us from destruction. If other means of communicating with us are not working, God may use dreams to bring about correction. I have received clear correction from the Lord in a dream a handful of times. Correction is such an important part of our development as God's children, and is necessary for us to stay on the right path in walking with God.

Third, we may experience *prophetic* dreams, in which God shows us something that will happen in the future for ourselves or someone else. There are a number of examples in scripture of prophetic dreams, specifically in the Old Testament with people like Daniel and Joseph. For example, in Genesis 37, 17-year-old Joseph has two dreams about the future that he shares with his father and brothers. His brothers resent him for his dreams because the interpretation suggests he will be promoted to such a high position that they will bow to him in honor. Maybe Joseph could have used discretion when sharing these dreams with his brothers, but in the end, the dreams were fulfilled and God accomplished his purpose.

I think God gives prophetic dreams for the same reason he gives prophetic words. Knowing what God is going to do causes us to pray, prepare, and stand with hope and courage when everything seems to oppose what we believe God has said. God gave me a prophetic dream concerning the local church I was to be a part of that has encouraged me to stand strong over the last 10 years.

The three categories of dreams that I suggested are not the only kind of dreams that God gives, but I have found them to be most common in scripture. Before closing the conversation on dreams I need to issue a warning. I have seen so many people get caught up in the details and obscure pieces of certain dreams they feel God has given them. Please hear me—God is not playing some cosmic game with us where he wants to see if we can put the obscure puzzle together. When a dream is not clear and needs interpretation, we must understand that only God can interpret the dream because he gave it in the first place. When nobody else could interpret Pharaoh's dream, they called upon Joseph, who replied, "It is not in me; God will give Pharaoh a favorable

When a dream is not clear and needs interpretation, we must understand that only God can interpret the dream because he gave it in the first place.

answer" (Gen. 41:16). The interpretation always belongs to God; he will reveal what he is trying to say to us when we ask him. If, as you pray, God doesn't reveal the answer to you, don't stress out about it; just be patient and wait for his answer.

Internal Voice

Sometimes we will hear God speak to us in our hearts and it very much comes across as a voice rather than just as thoughts. As we have discussed, the Holy Spirit lives inside of us, which is why hearing his *internal voice* will be more common than His *audible voice*. You may have heard others refer to this kind of communication as the "still small voice" of God, or maybe relate it to the work of human conscience. Either way, I prefer to call it the *internal voice* of the Holy Spirit instead of other terms.

When God speaks to me this way, I usually hear clear words, phrases, or sentences in my mind related to a situation or person that I have been thinking about. When I am on a long drive, in a quiet prayer time, or even in the middle of praying for someone, the Holy Spirit will say something like, "Tell Sam that I will provide finances if he takes the next step." The internal voice of the Holy Spirit will always be addressed to you, which will be a primary key in discerning that it is God and not just your own thoughts. You will typically hear things like "tell Ben this…," "my word says…," "read Psalm 91," or even "I love you."

One evening I was preparing a teaching for a church service I was going to speak at the following day. I was somewhat discouraged because I had discovered that some people I was in relationship with had been walking in secret sin for a while. To make matters worse, their poor choices came to light through even worse circumstances. Needless to say, this made my sermon preparation and prayer time interesting. I started writing a sermon about getting serious with the Lord and dealing with our sins before it's too late. Now, there is nothing wrong with that sermon for the most part, but the more I wrote, the less balanced it became. By that time it was getting late so I walked into my bathroom and started brushing my teeth. Without warning, in the middle of brushing, I heard the internal voice of the Spirit say, "Is that *your* experience of *me*?" Not only did I know that this was God, but I also knew exactly what he was saying to me by asking the question. I responded quickly with a broken heart, "No Lord, it's not my experience of you." My reaction to a grievous circumstance was about to become a sermon that misrepresented the full character of God to a group of people. As you can tell, I am so grateful for the internal voice of the Holy Spirit when he chooses to speak to me this way.

Audible Voice

I have read many books and listened to several testimonies from people who have claimed to hear the audible voice of God. Although I have experienced many supernatural things, I have never heard God's audible voice. I don't doubt for a second that some people have heard God this way. In his teenage years, a friend of mine was about to commit suicide and yet, in that very moment of decision, he heard the audible voice of God and consequently gave his life to Jesus. With this kind of dire situation, there is usually an urgency to the message God speaks, in which the person hearing needs an undeniable encounter with the voice of God.

Throughout the Bible there are examples of when God spoke audibly to people. The first one that comes to mind is in the story in 1 Samuel 3. Samuel was given to the priest Eli as a baby and was raised in the temple of the Lord. One day, while Samuel was lying down in the temple, he heard an audible voice call his name. Samuel, being a young man, assumed that this was the voice of Eli the Priest, because he did not yet know the voice of God. This was the beginning of Samuel hearing God speak to him; later, he would become a mighty prophet in Israel.

When Jesus was baptized in the Jordan River, several people nearby heard the audible voice of God (Luke 3:21-22). Before the Apostle Paul was converted, he was traveling to another town when all of a sudden a bright light flashed and he and his companions heard the audible voice of Jesus (Acts 9:3-7). While all of these examples were significant moments in history similar contemporary experiences carry the same level of seriousness. When God speaks to you audibly, he means to get your attention!

Angels

Just a quick Bible study demonstrates the profound role that angels play in the continually-unfolding plan of God. Most often, the literal definition of the word "angel" is actually "messenger."[13] Throughout the Bible, God's angels bring messages to people from the Lord. It seems to me that receiving a message from an angel is a very serious thing. While many people accept that receiving a message this way happened in ancient times, for some reason, the idea that this still happens today is largely disbelieved.

This experience happened with people like Abraham, Jacob, Moses, Gideon, Elijah, Mary, Joseph, and many others. As we read the book of Acts, there are several instances of angelic activity that should lead us to believe the same is still true today (e.g., Acts 8:26-27). Angels are still involved in human affairs as servants and messengers of God, and sometimes we are aware of them while other times we may not be (Heb. 13:2).

I have chosen to make a practice out of not discussing all of my encounters with the Lord, however, I will mention that I have personal experience with angelic messengers. At this point I have encountered direct angelic activity about six times. Most of these encounters were much like an open vision only stronger and obviously more impacting. When this first happened to me I began sharing about the experiences with people from my local church. Instead of excitement and interest, I was received with doubt and skepticism. Needless to say I was discouraged with the response then and have come to believe that such skepticism does not come from a biblical perspective but from a lack of experience. If we really believe the Bible is true then we should have no problem with the reality of angelic messengers.

I do want to emphasize the importance of weighing the source of every message, from wherever or whomever it comes, with the Bible. The Bible is the final authority for our lives and the enemy would love to send us down the wrong path. "No wonder, for even Satan disguises himself as an angel of light" (2 Cor. 11:14). As we seek to hear from God and accurately discern whatever may come across our paths, let's also be aware of God's messengers, for they play a special role alongside us for God's purposes.

Other People

All forms of communication we have discussed so far, except through angelic visitation, have to do with God speaking directly to us. While it is of utmost importance to cultivate a relationship with God that makes ongoing direct communication possible, we cannot overlook how God uses others to speak into our lives. As we grow in submission and accountability to one another, we find that God will often use the trusted voices of others to speak his counsel to us. When we don't allow other people to speak into our lives, it is often a sign that we are not allowing God to speak to us either. While each person is responsible to weigh the words of others through scripture, we must remember that the Holy Spirit lives in other people as well and will choose to speak through them sometimes.

There are probably countless ways that God will use people to speak his words to us, but there are a few that we will find to be most common. First, we may hear God speaking through others as they *teach* the Bible. Have you ever walked into a church service, heard a sermon, and then walked out with a new mindset concerning a particular

When we don't allow other people to speak into our lives, it is often a sign that we are not allowing God to speak to us either.

issue? This has happened to me several times. What happened? Well, because you were ready to receive, the Holy Spirit imparted something to you while someone was teaching the Bible. When someone is truly connected to God they will impart spiritual life to others as they exercise the teaching gift of the Holy Spirit (1 Pet. 4:11; Rom. 12:7).

The second way we will commonly hear God through others is in receiving *counsel.* I can't recall how many times I sought counsel from friends or pastors and God spoke through them exactly what I needed to hear. An encouraging passage I have used for some time is Proverbs 24:6 (NKJV): "For by wise counsel you will wage your own war, And in a multitude of counselors *there is* safety." There is wisdom in seeking the counsel of godly people, especially concerning things you are emotionally drained over (raising kids, marriage, job transition, ministry involvement, etc.).

The third common way we will hear God through others is *personal prophecy.* Prophecy is both a gift and function of the New Testament church (Acts 2:17-21). In 2003, I was pulled aside during a church service by a prophetic guy who told me I would write books! "Write books," I thought! I had never even written in a journal! I thought writing was for those passionate few that always dreamed of being writers. Even though I didn't resonate with his word that day, I couldn't shake it over the next few months and gradually started writing. Now, ten years later, I can't imagine what my life would be like without the discipline and joy of writing. New Testament prophecy is given to encourage, strengthen, and comfort God's church as we minister to one another (1 Cor. 14:3).

The Bottom Line

As we have looked at nine different ways that God may communicate with us, I hope it is understood that some of these we may never experience personally. Hearing God is what counts, so the way in which that happens is not as important. You may be wondering, "Why does God speak in so many different ways?" That is a great question, and I don't pretend to fully know the answer. I asked the Lord that question one day and in response I received a vision. In this vision I saw someone planting different seeds in their garden. As this person planted the different kinds of seeds (strawberries, lettuce, carrots, etc.), the seeds immediately became the fully-grown crop they were planted to be. When I awoke, I realized that God was showing me that, when he communicates with us, he plants his word in different ways (seeds) to achieve different results (fruit). Therefore, I have learned to trust that God knows both what I need to hear and *how* I need to hear it.

Chapter 4 Review Questions

1. What are the most common way(s) that you hear or have heard from God?

2. Do you think that you have been open or closed to other ways that God communicates?

3. In what way would you prefer to hear God speak to you? Why would you prefer this way?

4. What encouraged you most about this chapter and how will you apply it to your life?

CHAPTER 5
UNDERSTANDING WHY GOD SPEAKS

For a good portion of my Christian life I thought God only talked to me in order to tell me what to do. Some who do believe God speaks today also believe that "God doesn't speak to be heard; he speaks in order to be obeyed." Now I definitely believe this statement *contains* truth, but that doesn't mean it's the whole truth, so help us God!

The *why* behind God speaking to us is so much bigger than receiving marching orders from heaven. Surely there are things that God will say simply because he wants us to hear them: "I love you," "You're amazing," or "Good job." A good father would say such comments to his child, and Jesus said that God was a Good Father (Matt. 7:11). As a father, I am the same toward my kids, often saying things to them that are simply meant to affirm their identities, share my love, and praise their good choices.

In short, there are many different reasons that God will speak to us and we need to understand them as we progress in our discussion and understanding of hearing God's voice. For some of you, this chapter won't seem necessary, but there are many who will need to broaden their foundations to understand why God speaks so as not to miss what he might be saying.

I personally moved beyond a "God-only-speaks-to-be-obeyed" mindset to a "God-speaks-for-many-reasons" mindset after witnessing my brother and his wife dedicate their children to the Lord. The pastor prayed for my brother and his family and then began a sermon in keeping with what the church had been learning. Halfway into his sermon, the pastor gave an illustration of what God was like by using my brother's dedicating of his children as an example. The pastor said to my brother, "Young man, the Lord would say *thank-you*, and he wants you to know that he appreciates that you have dedicated your children to him. You didn't have to do that and he is proud that you did!"

I remember thinking, "God just wanted to say *thank-you?*" On the way home and even the following week, those words from the pastor stuck in my heart. God was showing me what kind of Father he truly is. Sure, I can see someone saying, "God doesn't say thank-you to anyone—that's unbiblical garbage." Okay, God doesn't need any of us, and he is totally secure in who he is, but that doesn't mean he won't say things to encourage us or show how proud he is of our decisions.

This experience opened my eyes to the many reasons that God speaks to us. Since then, I have encountered so many people who seem to only seek God's voice for that "thing" He wants them to do, often at the expense of many other things he says to them regularly. It's easy to get stuck in a weird place in which you want to hear from God, but miss all that God is saying because he isn't answering what you're asking about. God might not be speaking to you about your next world-changing event, but he could easily talk to you about your heart, your friends, or maybe he is talking to you about himself.

At twenty-one years old, while attending an evening service at my church, the Lord suddenly spoke to me very clearly: "I want you to help someone with a church in Kirkland." "What? Kirkland? Is that really you God?" These and other thoughts raced through my mind. The word was so clear it had to be God, but I had no idea what to do with it. Kirkland is a city located about 25 minutes from where I then lived at the time. I couldn't fathom moving to some unknown church in Kirkland.

Just a few months later I was attending another evening service during which our pastor introduced a man who was going to plant a church in the city of Kirkland. I won't lie; I started to sweat a little. While I could easily shrug off the word I had received for the last few months, I now had the connection and knew what I needed to do.

After the service I walked right up to the man and said, "Hi, my name is Ben, and I know you don't know me but God told me to help you with your church in Kirkland." The man said, "Great, you can just show up next Sunday at 7:00 a.m.," and I did. I spent the next couple years serving alongside these wonderful people at a church plant in the city of Kirkland.

During my time at the church I received mentoring from my pastor, friendship with many in our congregation, and tons of opportunities to lead in various ministry roles. It was an experience that I will never forget. During that time, God gave us many prophetic words for the church. In my heart I believed the church would grow, flourish, and change the city of Kirkland, but that did not come to pass. The church did not grow numerically and in some ways shrank from where we began.

About three years into the church plant the core leadership team prayed and felt that the Lord wanted us to close the doors. A few weeks later our wonderful church closed its doors and all of us spread out into various congregations. This decision was especially hard for our pastors who had given everything for the church and faced the question, as I did, "God, why did you have us do all this just to shut it all down?"

Initially, we all moved on to different places, different churches, and different lives. Over time, I began to wonder why God would tell me to help a church—and why in the first place he would tell my pastors to start a church in Kirkland—that he would close just three years later. I had assumed that God told us to do these things because he planned to use us to bring revival to Kirkland and see people saved, restored, and fall in love with Jesus.

I don't know the reasons that God told all of us to help with this church plant, but I now know what God wanted for me through this experience. The funny thing is that God's purpose had nothing to do with my impact or with being part of something that would bring revival to a city. This experience, personally, had to do with being mentored by an awesome family, getting my feet wet in vocational ministry, serving the needs that were in front of me, and trusting God no matter what happened. When God spoke to me about going to this church I initially thought it was about obeying God for impact, but I later learned it was about trusting God for personal growth.

My journey helped me understand that God doesn't speak to us just to tell us what to do. Even when it seems he is telling us what to do, he may have completely different purposes in mind than what we expect. While we may never know all the reasons God speaks to us, developing a broader perspective for why God will speak to you is important. God develops this perspective in us over time, through experience, as we seek to hear his voice and understand what and why he has spoken along the way. Overall, this journey has imparted to me a deeper understanding and appreciation for hearing God's voice.

God Makes Himself Known

The first and most important reason that God speaks to us is to make himself known. One of the amazing attributes of God is that he is omniscient, which means he knows everything about us including our past, present, and future. We can go even further by saying that God knows more about each one of us than we know about ourselves. There are many examples of God's omniscience in scripture but one of the more famous passages is the call of the Prophet Jeremiah.

> Now the word of the Lord came to me saying, "Before I formed you in the womb I knew you, And before you were

born I consecrated you; I have appointed you a prophet to the
nations. (Jer. 1:4-5)

Jeremiah was likely in his late teens when he received this call
from God. Essentially, the Lord called Jeremiah, in his youth, to be a
prophet to the nations. In this passage the Lord shared with Jeremiah
that, while this call was new to him, God had known all along. God
knew Jeremiah before he was born and set him apart even before he
had been given a name. This is profound considering the depth of
God's knowledge of our own lives and futures.

King David wrote a Psalm that reflects upon God's infinite knowledge.

O LORD, You have searched me and known *me*. You
know when I sit down and when I rise up; You understand my
thought from afar. You scrutinize my path and my lying down,
And are intimately acquainted with all my ways. Even before
there is a word on my tongue, Behold, O LORD, You know
it all. You have enclosed me behind and before, And laid Your
hand upon me. *Such* knowledge is too wonderful for me; It is
too high, I cannot attain to it. (Ps. 139:1-6)

Can you even fathom the depth to which God knows you? God
intimately knows every cell of your body, every hair on your head, every
word you will speak, every place you will live, every child you will have,
and every difficulty you will face. Friends, God knows us to such a degree
that we are quickly overwhelmed trying to imagine it, like King David
who said, "Such knowledge is too wonderful for me" (Ps. 139:6).

God knows us, but something is still lacking; we don't know Him.
The truth is we will never know God to the degree that he knows us
because it's not possible. However, God still wants to make himself
known to us and he does this primarily by speaking to us. Let's be clear:
we are not talking about book knowledge, but about true personal
knowledge that can only be shared by relational experience. God created us to *know* Him, not just know about Him.

In the book of Exodus God used a man named Moses to deliver the nation of Israel from slavery and lead them to a new land of blessing. Prior to entering this Promised Land, God led Israel through a wilderness with many difficult obstacles that would be useful in bringing them into a revelation of who God really is.

I personally think that the wilderness experience had a lot to do with God's desire to make himself known to Moses and Israel because they didn't really know him before. Moses clearly had a special relationship with God because of the kind of uncommon communication they shared. "Thus the LORD used to speak to Moses face to face, just as a man speaks to his friend..." (Exod. 33:11). God revealed himself to Moses unlike anyone

When God speaks to us he reveals his character and love toward us, which will remove many of our preconceived notions and cause our love for Him to grow stronger.

else in his day. This kind of relationship ignited something in Moses' heart to want to know God even more.

> Then Moses said to the LORD, "See, You say to me, 'Bring up this people!' But You Yourself have not let me know whom You will send with me. Moreover, You have said, 'I have known you by name, and you have also found favor in My sight.' Now therefore, I pray You, if I have found favor in Your sight, let me know Your ways that I may know You, so that I may find favor in Your sight. Consider too, that this nation is Your people." (Exod. 33:12-13)

In this conversation Moses says to God, "You know me and my ways, so let me know *you* and *your ways*." After walking with God for some time and having the privilege of hearing his voice regarding directions and commandments, Moses just wanted God to show him who he was and what he was like. Knowing God is a human being's deepest desire. God will speak to us in many ways throughout our lives to make himself known.

So often we think God is one way or another based on what we were taught in church or by the example of others. When God speaks to us he reveals his character and love toward us, which will remove many of our preconceived notions and cause our love for Him to grow stronger.

God Reveals Our Purpose in His Plan

God has a plan that involves every person, especially those who believe upon Jesus and walk with him in the partnership of the gospel. As we have discussed, God knows everything about us including our futures, which involves the roles we each play in his unfolding plan for humanity. That's right, you have a significant role in what God is doing today and he wants to make you aware of the assignments he has for you specifically.

How do we know what God wants us to do in this life? Generally speaking, we know what God wants based on the scriptures. However, we are made aware of the specific things that God has called us to do when he speaks to us in the various ways we have discussed. For example, I received a prophetic word that I would write books. As I spent time with God, he confirmed the same word to my heart. For me, writing books in order to equip the Body of Christ is one of the specific things that God has called me to do.

In the beginning of what would prove to be a very difficult time for Israel, the Prophet Jeremiah gave a prophetic word for the nation that carries truth for us as well. "For I know the plans that I have for you,' declares the Lord, 'plans for welfare and not for calamity to give you a future and a hope'" (Jer. 29:11). Regardless of what Israel's circumstance looked like at the time of receiving this word, God knew what was going to happen and how the people of Israel still had a purpose in his plan.

God knows the plan and no matter what it looks like right now, he has a word of hope to speak over us as we partner with him to accomplish his will and plan throughout our lives. Our situation may not seem like God has any great plan for us, but he does! What has God told you to do? What are the purposes of God that you are to accomplish? Regardless of what others have said or what you have told yourself, God has special things for you to do in this life! I have noticed that the Lord has no problem saying to people things that stretch far beyond where they find themselves in life, things that are much greater than what they themselves could ever accomplish. Our job is not to question the Lord but rather to hear him and believe what he says, no matter what!

God does not want us to be ignorant of the things he has called us to do, but sometimes we are. I think the ignorance about our purposes in God's plan is often the result of our failure to ask him for specifics. Some time ago I was praying and asking the Lord what he wanted me to focus on and he spoke to me about the importance of audio and video resources for our ministry. This was not something that I had previously considered, nor did I know how to bring any of it about. Nevertheless, God had called me to have a

I think the ignorance about our purposes in God's plan is often the result of our failure to ask him for specifics.

discipleship presence in parts of the world I was never to visit. He spoke to me about *how* that would happen and I simply followed his direction. So, we began by recording all of our teachings, and things took off from there. Today, I may teach a class with 150 people in attendance, but because we launched audio and video resources as the Lord directed, we have ten to twenty times that amount watching and listening to us online from all over the world.

When the apostle Paul wrote to the Ephesian church he wanted them to know how incredible they were in God's eyes:

> For by grace you have been saved through faith; and that
> not of yourselves, *it is* the gift of God; not as a result of works,
> so that no one may boast. For we are His workmanship, created
> in Christ Jesus for good works, which God prepared before-
> hand so that we would walk in them. (Eph. 2:8-10)

By God's grace, we are called to do significant things, which God has known about and made preparation for even before we were born. Our job is to walk with God and listen to what he tells us to do so that we might embrace the specific assignments for which he has already made plans.

Only God knows the whole picture and he usually chooses to only give us one piece at a time. Have you ever bought or been given a puzzle of some kind? While I am not a fan of puzzles I can remember working on a few when I was younger. I wonder what it would be like to work on a twenty-thousand-piece puzzle with no picture of what it should look like when you finish. Pointless, I'm sure! Life is like that puzzle and only God knows what the whole picture looks like in the end. In the journey of life we need to hear God about what pieces to put down and trust him as the whole thing comes together over time. It's really his plan, but it's our privilege to have a purpose in the midst of it, and our responsibility to hear and obey no matter what he might say.

God Brings Us Back to the Narrow Path

Another reason that God speaks to us is to bring correction to something. Unfortunately, most people think of correction as a bad thing, which couldn't be farther from the truth. We need God's voice of correction if we are going to stay on the narrow path and not end up in a ditch. I can't tell you how many times the Lord has given me one word of correction and literally saved me years of difficulty, incredible pain, and unnecessary relational conflict.

As discussed, when we become Christians our direction in life comes under new leadership. We become followers of Jesus, no longer following ourselves or any one else. We quickly notice that all the voices don't go away just because we've said "yes" to Jesus. Sometimes we sin and make really poor decisions based on following the leadership of the flesh, but God is faithful to lead us back to the path of life so we don't stay stuck in destructive patterns.

God corrects us because he loves us and wants the very best for our lives. Whenever God points out the truth in order to correct the way we think or the things we are doing, we should welcome it with open arms. The word "correct" simply means to set right again, to make paths straight, to rebuke, or to point out error. Although we are born again and made new by God's Spirit, our minds are not yet fully renewed (Rom. 12:1-2); thus, not all of our choices are from God. Therefore, we need God's loving, fatherly voice of correction to reveal the right way and the right choice, in contrast to what we may be thinking or doing.

It baffles me how so many people talk or act like God has no interest in bringing correction to their lives. If one of my children starts making sinful choices that will lead to an inevitable hardship if continued, I will be the first to speak to them about it in the hope that I might save them from future pain. God's correc-

God's correction imparts the right direction!

tion is not about punishment; it's about keeping us on the path that we were created for, the path of life.

The Bible is the primary voice of God in our lives and we see clearly that one of the main purposes of scripture is to provide correction in order to shape us.

> All Scripture is inspired by God and profitable for teaching, for reproof, *for correction*, for training in righteousness; so that the man of God may be adequate, equipped for every good work. (2 Tim. 3:16-17)

The correction of scripture helps us move away from what's wrong and step into what's right. The goal of God's correction is not just to make us feel bad for the wrong, but to help us become who he created us to be all along. God's correction imparts the right direction!

When King Solomon wrote the Proverbs he clearly had his sons in mind (Prov. 1:8; 2:1; 3:1; 4:1; 5:1; 6:1). He wrote straightforward truths for his children and others so that they could avoid destruction and cling to true wisdom, which leads to life. Solomon made many comments about the importance of correction and our role in receiving it. He also mentioned that those who don't receive correction are lazy, foolish, bad leaders, stupid, and will end up harming themselves and others (his words, not mine).

> Whoever heeds discipline shows the way to life, but whoever ignores correction leads others astray. (Prov. 10:17, NIV)

> Whoever loves discipline loves knowledge, but whoever hates correction is stupid. (Prov. 12:1, NIV)

> Whoever disregards discipline comes to poverty and shame, but whoever heeds correction is honored (Prov. 13:18, NIV)

> A fool spurns a parent's discipline, but whoever heeds correction shows prudence. (Prov. 15:5, NIV)

> Mockers resent correction, so they avoid the wise. (Prov. 15:12, NIV)
> Stern discipline awaits anyone who leaves the path; the one who hates correction will die. (Prov. 15:10, NIV)

I am not saying that we need to jump up and down in excitement for God's correction, but we *must* be aware that it plays an important role in our development as his children. It is a loving act on God's part to speak correction when we need it so we can stay on or get on the right path. To perceive God's voice of correction any other way than loving is simply inaccurate.

Receiving correction from the Lord is all about humility of heart. I encourage you to trust the Lord Jesus as you follow him and know that whatever he says to you is for your good. Corrective words will not be as hard to hear when we trust the one speaking and know the potential it has in transforming many areas of our lives.

God Wants to Speak through Us

As it is with everything in the Christian life, God often gives us something so that we might give it to others. While I have spent the majority of this book talking about hearing God for your own life, it is important to discuss, even briefly, hearing God for others, yet another reason that God speaks to us personally.

Prophecy occurs when God speaks to us about someone else and we share what he has told us with that person. The issue of prophecy is not a small subject in the Bible and truly deserves a thorough study, for which I recommend my book on the gift of prophecy.

Prophecy occurs when God speaks to us about someone else and we share what he has told us with that person.

When I first started hearing the voice of God I had never heard of the term "prophecy" outside of a conversation regarding the end times or eschatology. However, the experience of prophecy became normal for me even during my first year of walking with Jesus. Sometimes I would stand next to someone in church, the grocery store, or the movie theater, and all of a sudden I'd begin receiving pictures, thoughts, or scriptures relevant for that person. Receiving the revelation is important, but God intends for us to bless and strengthen the person with his words.

In order to help them in their use of spiritual gifts, the Apostle Paul writes to the Corinthian church about the purpose and benefit of prophetic words.

> Pursue love, yet desire earnestly spiritual *gifts*, but especially that you may prophesy. For one who speaks in a tongue does not speak to men but to God; for no one understands, but in *his* spirit he speaks mysteries. But one who prophesies speaks to men for edification and exhortation and consolation. One who speaks in a tongue edifies himself; but one who prophesies edifies the church. Now I wish that you all spoke in tongues, but *even* more that you would prophesy; and greater is one who prophesies than one who speaks in tongues, unless he interprets, so that the church may receive edifying. (1 Cor. 14:1-5)

Paul mentions that we should have a strong desire for spiritual gifts, but especially prophecy. Why? When a person hears a prophetic word from a brother or sister they are encouraged, strengthened, and comforted with God's thoughts toward them. What a profound privilege to hear God's voice for others and to share with them what God is saying!

You may be saying, "I don't have the gift of prophecy," or "That's not how God uses me!" Well, the Apostle Paul told us to desire prophecy, not for ourselves, but to strengthen others. If the Holy Spirit lives inside of us and knows everything about every person on the planet, I don't think it's a big deal for Him to share something with us that will help another person. In fact, I think God loves to share things with us for others when he knows we will truly use that information for their benefit and not our own.

As I have said before, God is speaking to us all the time but we often aren't receiving what He is saying. When you know that God will speak to you for others, in any context, it helps you to receive from him and it gives you confidence to share what you have heard. When I first started receiving words from the Lord for people I rarely shared them because I really didn't understand what prophecy was, what it was for, or if what I was receiving was even from God. However, once I learned that God sometimes gives us his words for others, the more intentional I became in sharing those words.

A long time ago, one of my friends was at the end of his rope, tired of destroying his life. He went down to the local restaurant by himself to consider his life—no money, no job, no hope, and no life. While sitting in the restaurant drinking a cup of coffee, a man walked up to his table and sat down across from him. The man said "Son, Jesus loves you and he wanted me to tell you that." After saying this, the man invited my friend to a church service where my friend gave his whole heart to Jesus Christ. The prophetic word wasn't detailed and may not sound very prophetic, but to my friend it was a word from God in his situation. One word from God can change a person's life. You can be the vessel that God uses to share such a word. My friends, when God speaks something to you that is meant for somebody else, be courageous and speak up!

My friends, when God speaks something to you that is meant for somebody else, be courageous and speak up!

Chapter 5 Review Questions

1. Have you ever overlooked what God is saying to you because you are looking for him to say something else? How does it help to know the different reasons that God communicates to us?

2. Have you resisted the correction of God in your life? If so, why do you think that is?

3. Does God ever speak to you about other people? How is the frequency of hearing God for others related to the frequency of asking God for others? How will you pursue this more effectively?

4. What encouraged you most about this chapter and how will you apply it to your life?

CHAPTER 6
HINDRANCES TO HEARING GOD

When I was about nine years old I was outside in our cul-de-sac playing baseball with all the neighborhood kids. For some reason I got stuck being the catcher for our first game. How I hated playing that position! Not long into the game one of my friends stepped up to the plate and, as the ball was pitched, he took one step back and swung for a home run. I still have no idea why he took a step back, but instead of hitting a home run, he swung the bat against the right side of my head, sending me straight to the ground. With the help of a few people I got up and headed home so my mom could take me to the hospital. Fortunately for me, my jaw and skull were intact, but my right ear was severely damaged. I remember waking up in the morning with a constant ringing in my ear that has never fully gone away. Even to this day, I have a measure of hearing impairment in my right ear that I have learned to live with.

Since that day I have dealt with ongoing hearing problems whose symptoms come and go. One month I can hear fine, and the next month I hear about fifty percent out of my right ear. When I was hit, my ear was damaged in its ability to drain fluid, making it difficult to hear whenever I have water in my middle ear that will not drain. It's beyond annoying and the frequent ear infections affect many of life's activities. Apart from a creative miracle, which I am still praying for, my hearing may decline as the years go by and I could end up being the old guy who walks around yelling, "Huh, what did you say?"

While the complications that I live with are minor compared to a deaf person, I still understand to some degree what it means to be hearing impaired. I am often engaged in a conversation wherein I can't fully hear what the speaker is saying, and I just say "yeah" and shake my head like I heard the whole thing. I have accepted the fact that the problem is my hearing and not the speaking, so instead of asking for an accommodation to my impairment by speaking on my left side, or speaking a little louder, I usually just go with the flow and receive from the conversation what I can. Awesome, right? Just so you know, this is our secret so don't tell anybody! I have learned, like so many others, to adapt to life without a normal hearing ability.

Not everyone will experience hindrances to their physical hearing, but at some point all of us will encounter hindrances in hearing from God. There are many reasons why we may not be hearing from God, but like my physical hearing, the issue is never with the one speaking. In the different gospel accounts, Jesus told many stories to the crowds about the Kingdom of God. At the end of some of these stories, Jesus would say, "He who has ears to hear, let him hear!" (Mark 4:9; Luke 8:8; 14:35) Have you ever wondered why Jesus said this? I sure have. Obviously, the people that Jesus was speaking to had physical ears, but that doesn't mean they understood or received his words. The question for every follower of Jesus is, "Do I have ears to hear what Jesus is saying to me?"

A hindrance is something that will prevent or stop us from hearing what God is saying. Since we are created to hear and follow God, it is extremely important to take every hindrance as a serious threat to our growth and overall well-being. In fact, when we are hindered from hearing God, we are also hindered from obeying God. Jesus said, "My sheep hear My voice, and I know them, and they follow Me" (John 10:27). For Christians, obedience should be the natural outflow of hearing, which is why we must not be hindered as we seek to hear God.

As we look at various hindrances we may experience, it's important to keep our hearts fixed on the one and only solution: Jesus. When Jesus died on the cross and rose from the dead, he demolished every hindrance to hearing our Father's voice (Eph. 2:13). God's cell phone has full bars; if ours doesn't then we must recognize that it's our own equipment and not our Service Provider (Jesus).

We Don't Know God

For the last ten or so years I have been fortunate enough to serve as a prayer team member in our local church. I love to pray and consider it a privilege to stand beside someone in a moment of need as we seek God's answer together. In praying with many people I have made the basic mistake of assuming everyone who requests prayer during a church service is already a Christian. I must admit, to my shame, that I repeatedly made this mistake for several years.

After a church service one day, I walked to the front and joined the prayer teams for a time of ministry. One gentleman came to me and began sharing a current struggle he was walking through. I listened to him for a few minutes and then began to pray and wait on the Lord. While praying I felt like something was not quite right but I had no idea what it was so I didn't pay special attention to it. I finished the prayer and we talked for a moment. Right before the man left he made a comment about how he doesn't hear God or feel like he knows him. I asked the man, "When did you give your life to Jesus?" to which he promptly replied, "I don't know that I have." Really? Did this really just happen to me? For the last ten minutes I was praying with someone who wanted to hear God and the whole time his problem was that he just didn't know God.

I learned two things from this experience. First, I will never again assume that someone is a Christian just because they're at church or because they have come to the front for prayer. Second, the greatest hindrance to hearing from God is to not know God personally. To hear God is to know God and knowing God will position you to hear him.

Remember, Jesus said that his sheep hear his voice (John 10:27). Furthermore, Jesus spelled it out clearly to the Jewish religious leaders during a heated discussion about his own identity. "He who is of God hears the words of God; for this reason you do not hear *them,* because you are not of God" (John 8:47). They were hindered from hearing God both through Jesus and the scriptures because they were not true followers of God.

> **To hear God is to know God and knowing God will position you to hear him.**

I am sure that most of you reading this book are committed to the Lord Jesus. However, if you have not submitted your life to Jesus Christ, I encourage you to receive his love right now. You might be saying, "I don't hear God at all," and in this moment I am asking you, is Jesus your Shepherd? Are you following Jesus or have you been following your own voice? Have you given your life to Jesus Christ and received forgiveness for your sins through his death and resurrection? If not, let this be a word from God to you: he wants to know you personally and communicate with you in a deeply relational way. You will hear God's voice, but it all starts with making a decision to follow Jesus with your whole heart.

Neglecting Time with God

When I first became a Christian I loved spending countless hours with the Lord in prayer and Bible study. Being nineteen and single afforded me the opportunity to spend many hours with the Lord; it didn't feel like much of a sacrifice. With the passing of each year and the increase of responsibility, those hours with God can easily turn into minutes if you're not careful.

Undoubtedly, relationship with God is unique in many ways, but we can easily draw some similarities from the relationship between spouses. Every good relationship has good communication. Whenever my wife and I facilitate pre- or post-marriage counseling, we are quickly reminded that the quality of communication in a relationship determines the quality of that relationship as a whole. That said, a husband and wife cannot have good communication without spending meaningful and consistent time together. This truth is the same in relationship with God.

As Christians, one of the greatest hindrances to hearing God speak is our failure to spend quality time with him.

As Christians, one of the greatest hindrances to hearing God speak is our failure to spend quality time with him. This is probably not news to you, but I hope that we all truly understand that neglecting time with God is even more serious than neglecting time with our spouses. God should have first place in our lives—when that is not the case we will be hindered in hearing him.

It's tragic that Christians know more about sports than about the Bible, and that the average American spends two to three hours per day watching television, while only five (or fewer) minutes in daily prayer. At some point we just need to connect the dots and admit that we don't hear God because we don't spend time with God because we spend all of our time doing everything else. It's equally tragic when we spend most of our time doing things for God without spending any time with God.

When I was a youth pastor I attended a leader's luncheon at one of the larger churches in the area. During our time together, the speaker asked us to write down the average minutes we spent in prayer per day. When everybody finished, we folded our papers and handed them to an usher who went away to tally the results. A few minutes later, the speaker was handed the results. As he read them to us, to my surprise, the majority of youth pastors spent less than five minutes in prayer per day. I will never forget the look on all of our faces when the speaker said, "Is that really going to cut it for your life with God and your ministry to his people?" Without a word, over one hundred youth pastors in the room said "No!" in unison.

While I didn't walk away from that meeting with shame, I did leave with a sober perspective that I myself had accepted less time with God as the norm, and that was no longer okay with me. I don't care if I am a pastor, have a ministry, or if people know my name, but I do care if I place everything in my life before God and yet, for some odd reason, expect good communication from Him. We don't expect that a marital relationship to be good without quality time, so we shouldn't expect any different with the Lord. We are, after all, his Bride. It is eternally true that the more time we spend with him, the more we will hear from him.

During a visit with his friends Martha and Mary, Jesus spoke to the issue of neglecting time with God.

> Now as they were traveling along, He entered a village; and a woman named Martha welcomed Him into her home. She had a sister called Mary, who was seated at the Lord's feet, *listening to His word*. But Martha was *distracted with all her preparations*; and she came up *to Him* and said, "Lord, do You not care that my sister has left me to do all the serving alone? Then tell her to help me." But the Lord answered and said to her, "Martha, Martha, you are worried and bothered about so many things; but *only* one thing is necessary, for Mary has chosen the good part, which shall not be taken away from her." (Luke 10:38-42)

We see a picture of two women making two very different decisions about the most important moment of their lives. The Bible says that Mary was sitting at the Lord's feet "listening to [Jesus]," while Martha was in the background, busy with all the preparations. Martha confronted the Lord about Mary's choice because she thought it was laziness that caused her sister to sit on the floor at Jesus's feet. Jesus quickly pointed out that the most important thing she could do was the very thing that Mary was doing, "sitting at his feet, listening to His word." Jesus did not say that what Martha was doing was unimportant; he was explaining that it wasn't as important.

Why do we believe that when our schedules lighten up, or this season of life calms down, we will then be able to get to the important stuff, like more time with God? It's a lie. There will always be things to do, places to go, and people to help. While all these things need to get done, and surely are important, if God is not first in our lives, then everything else doesn't matter much. The simple truth is that we are hindered in hearing from God when we neglect spending time with God.

A Hard Heart

I wish my Christian life had a perfect track record, but that has honestly not been the case. When I first became a Christian, I was delivered from every major struggle that I was aware of: drugs, alcohol, and sexual promiscuity. My experience was a true heart transplant; Jesus took my heart of stone and replaced it with a heart of flesh (Ezek. 11:17-21). I was a new person and it was so powerful that I hardly remember experiencing any temptation to sin for the first six months. Oh but the season for escaping temptation was short, and I was soon again tempted by the same sins that I had been delivered from.

Although I was truly new and experienced supernatural deliverance, I ended up going back to a certain sin and my heart began to harden again. During this time, while sitting in a meeting in church, I felt convicted by the speaker's sermon, but I refused to respond. I needed God's help and the help of others to lead me to repentance. The longer I didn't respond the harder my heart became. I knew my secret sin was wrong. I knew I needed to change and I even wanted to change, but becoming humble and honest about everything seemed too costly for some reason.

I would stay up late at night with my Bible open, so desperately wanting to hear from God, when all the while God was speaking to me through conviction, which I was ignoring. I searched the Bible to find relief for my struggles, but God wouldn't let me move on. I learned firsthand how deceitful sin could be. Closing our spiritual ears to the Holy Spirit's conviction will keep us from hearing *all* of the things God is saying.

Closing our spiritual ears to the Holy Spirit's conviction will keep us from hearing *all* of the things God is saying.

One day, I decided to go to a friend's house to confess my sin and get right with God. My heart was softened as I responded to the Spirit's conviction and I began hearing the wonderful voice of God with great clarity. If we choose to live in unrepentant sin, eventually our hearts will harden and hearing God will significantly decrease. Refusing to listen and respond to the conviction of the Holy Spirit will eventually make us spiritually hard of hearing, because hearing God is about the condition of your heart. The principle is always true that a hardened heart will cause hardness of hearing.

Listen to the warnings from the writer of Hebrews conveyed to a struggling people in the first century.

> Take care, brethren, that there not be in any one of you an evil, unbelieving heart that falls away from the living God. But encourage one another day after day, as long as it is *still* called "Today," so that none of you will be *hardened by the deceitfulness of sin.* For we have become partakers of Christ, if we hold fast the beginning of our assurance firm until the end, while it is said, *"TODAY IF YOU HEAR HIS VOICE, DO NOT HARDEN YOUR HEARTS, AS WHEN THEY PROVOKED ME."* For who provoked *Him* when they had heard? Indeed, did not all those who came out of Egypt *led* by Moses? And with whom was He angry for forty years? Was it not with those who sinned, whose bodies fell in the wilderness? And to whom did He swear that they

would not enter His rest, but to those who were disobedient? (Heb. 3:12-18)

This passage makes it clear that we can be "hardened by the deceit-
fulness of sin," through which we resist what God is saying, and the
writer mentions that the people of Israel also struggled with this during
the time of the Exodus. I know from experience that it takes courage
to humble oneself before the Lord and others, but I also know how
central it is to experiencing true freedom in Christ. When we humble
ourselves, God gives us the grace to live victoriously in the same areas
we were once defeated (Jas. 4:6-10). If the Lord is convicting you of
something, do not seek another word; instead, humble yourself and
get your heart right with him and you will begin hearing his voice
more clearly.

Only Special People Hear from God

Another typical hindrance is summed up in the phrase, "God only
talks to special or really spiritual people." This perspective is wrong in so
many ways. Usually when people have this perspective, they imply that
they are not one of those "special people" that God talks to. Let's be clear;
everybody is flawed. Everybody needs the blood of Jesus to cover their
sins—yes, everybody! You can't earn the privilege of hearing from God because it's a central part of the relationship for which Jesus gave his life. If we believe that God only speaks to special people, then we also believe that God plays favorites with his kids, which is simply untrue.

It is possible to live in such a way that we don't hear God's voice and then choose to use the "I'm-not-real-spiritual" excuse. Sure, if you don't spend time with God, or if you keep a secret life of sin, you probably won't hear God's voice much, but that is on you, not God. While God does give each one different assignments and callings, He doesn't choose favorites regarding whom he will or won't talk to.

In considering those God speaks to, let's look at what James says in his letter.

> But if any of you lacks wisdom, let him ask of God, who gives to all generously and without reproach, and it will be given to him. But he must ask in faith without any doubting, for the one who doubts is like the surf of the sea, driven and tossed by the wind. For that man ought not to expect that he will receive anything from the Lord, *being* a double-minded man, unstable in all his ways. (Jas. 1:5-8)

In his letter, James wrote that when we lack wisdom, all we need to do is *ask God*. How does God give us wisdom? He speaks to us. In other words, when we ask God for wisdom, we are asking him to communicate with us about what we should do in a present circumstance. The only prerequisite that I see in this passage is that the person who asks must do so in faith, meaning they must believe that God will give them what they ask for. This is the exact opposite of the "you-have-to-be-special-or-spiritual" perspective. Later in James we read of the very reason that we don't have wisdom—we don't ask for it (Jas. 4:2).

You may recall that Jesus taught the same thing about asking in Matthew 7:7-8.

> Ask, and it will be given to you; seek, and you will find; knock, and it will be opened to you. For everyone who asks receives, and he who seeks finds, and to him who knocks it will be opened.

The truth is that some hear God more than others because they ask more often, not because they are somehow more special. God doesn't play favorites but he does respond to those who ask. Maybe we're not hearing the voice of God often because we don't ask him to speak to us very often.

Hearing God Is a Spiritual Gift

When I started writing about hearing from God I made the decision to write two books. The first book is the one you are reading, and the second book is solely focused on the gift of prophecy. Part of the reason I made this decision was because of the confusion between hearing God for ourselves (relational communication), and hearing God for others (prophetic gifts and ministry).

> # Hearing God for your own life is based out of your relationship, not a spiritual gifting for ministry.

Hearing God for your own life is based out of your relationship, not a spiritual gifting for ministry. Jesus made it clear that everyone who knows him should hear his voice. "My sheep hear My voice, and I know them, and they follow Me" (John 10:27). Prophecy occurs when we hear God for someone else and share it with them. Therefore, prophecy is defined by speaking to others what one has heard from God. The difference is important, especially as we read the Bible and define terms such as prophecy, prophets, etc.

You don't have to be a prophet or possess the gift of prophecy to hear God speak to you. God loves you and wants to communicate with you in deep and meaningful ways that have nothing to do with others' spiritual gifts. When somebody looks at hearing from God only as a spiritual gift, they usually think they can't hear God and automatically cut themselves off from growing in a real relationship with God that involves communication.

This hindrance is based on certain teachings regarding spiritual gifts that I do not personally agree with. I believe that everyone can hear God *and* everyone can prophesy (Acts 2:17-21; 1 Cor. 14:1). It's unfortunate that many of us have heard teachings that limit what God does in and through us. If you have somehow blocked the issue of hearing from God because of past teachings on spiritual gifts, then I encourage you to examine the difference in hearing God for yourself and hearing God for others. Additionally, I would encourage you to further evaluate any teaching on spiritual gifts that somehow restricts the ministry of the Spirit through you.

Deceived by the Enemy

As we will discuss more in chapter 7, "Discerning God's Voice," the enemy seeks to deceive us in order to stop the spreading of God's kingdom through our lives. I don't think anybody wants to be deceived and those who are don't think that they are because that is the very nature of deception.

There are two ways that deception prevents us from hearing God. The first and most prevalent way is through false teaching. The Apostle Paul warned Timothy several times about false teaching and exhorted him to stand strong in sound doctrine (1 Tim. 4:6). Paul even went as far as saying that some people would be deceived by following "doctrines of demons." "[T]he Spirit explicitly says that in later times some will fall away from the faith, paying attention to deceitful spirits and doctrines of demons" (1 Tim. 4:1). There are demonic spirits that are devoted to promoting false teaching in order to confuse and mislead the Body of Christ. False teaching creates a ripple effect with what we believe about other important truths. A deceived person always thinks they are right and everybody else is wrong, so their mission becomes to enlighten everyone else. The sad reality is that they are wrong because what they *believe* is wrong. No matter how hard you try to show them clear Bible passages, they don't have eyes to see it.

As I minister in different churches I meet many people. It shocks me how some teachings will skew others' ability to hear from God. A few years ago, I was invited to minister at a church for a special conference weekend. I had never been to the church before nor did I know anyone from the church before coming. Shortly after arriving, I entered the prayer room to seek God before the services started. During prayer I kept feeling uncomfortable with what others were praying, and how they were representing the voice of God through prophetic words. After our prayer time, my friend and I engaged in conversation with one of the intercessors who was clearly confused. He began telling us that several people from the church had told him he didn't really need the Bible because God would speak to him directly.

No wonder we were discerning so many odd things during our time with this church. They had bought into a false teaching that the Holy Spirit would be their only Guide, supplanting the Bible which is serious error. We spent some time trying to help this person understand the importance of the Bible and how God establishes things by his word and gives specifics by his Spirit. This false teaching was not only hindering people from hearing God, it was also opening them to all kinds

Deception, like cancer, won't stop growing until it consumes and eventually destroys the whole body.

of other deceptive teachings and prophecies. Deception, like cancer, won't stop growing until it consumes and eventually destroys the whole body. Knowing, studying, loving, and staying devoted to the word of God will keep us from an incredible amount of deception.

Another way we can be deceived and hindered from hearing the voice of God is through false prophecy. First of all, we should never take what somebody else says as the whole truth, because we also have the Bible and the Holy Spirit to help us understand and interpret words of prophecy. We should consider and pray about what others may say to us, even when they claim to have heard from God, because *they* are not God, so their words need to be weighed carefully regardless of how accurate they may be.

I have listened to at least five people tell me they believe the Lord gave them confirmation to divorce their spouses, but without any biblical basis whatsoever. No matter what I said, I couldn't talk them out of it. When someone receives a false word as truth, that person is deceived and thus hindered from hearing God. "I am supposed to leave this church." "God has called me to stop working and do ministry full time." "The Lord told me that I am not suppose to reconcile because the other person will come to me first." I have heard all of these claims, and so many more. False prophecies are not always evil or demonic, but if they do not conform to the Bible, they are still not from God. Again, a lot of these kinds of words could easily be discarded when discerned through the truth of the Bible.

If we hear from the Lord for others, we need to be careful that what we hear and speak is grounded in scripture and truly from the Holy Spirit. It grieves me to see people communicate on behalf of the Lord when it's really something that they are *feeling* from their own emotions, rather than something they are *hearing* from the Lord. The enemy is not always the one deceiving us; sometimes it's our emotional condition that leads us to think if we feel a certain way that God must feel the same way. In the Old Testament, God rebuked people for speaking false words that came from their own minds (Jer. 14:14). We should be careful that what we are hearing and speaking is truly coming from God because if it's not we can be deceived and hindered from what God is really saying.

Religious Pride

When we have religious pride we tend to override the voice of God by not welcoming the voice of others or of God. We think we already have everything figured out. A prideful person may still want to hear God, and even act like God has spoken. However, that person's mind is really doing the talking. Pride is the devil's nature and was the essence of his downfall (Isa. 14:12-14). When we are prideful we take on the nature of the enemy and live in opposition to the voice of God. "But He gives a greater grace. Therefore *it* says, 'GOD IS OPPOSED TO THE PROUD, BUT GIVES GRACE TO THE HUMBLE'" (Jas. 4:6).

As a pastor, there are times where I am required to give correction to someone in order to bring about awareness and change. One day I met with an individual to prayerfully discuss some pretty big insights I had into their character and behavior. As we were talking, the Lord gave me a vision of an envelope being given to them. While receiving the envelope, the person quickly stamped the top "return to sender" and promptly gave it back. The vision ended and my eyes were opened to the pride of the individual sitting before me.

The rest of our conversation completely reflected the vision that the Lord gave me. Although this person listened to what I had to say, they could not hear me because their pride was in the way. I walked away from that meeting very grieved because I knew their response toward me was just a reflection of their response toward God.

Proud people don't ask for the help or counsel of others, including God's. This kind of life leads to destruction (Prov. 16:18). We will destroy our potential, our destinies, and our very purposes without God's counsel in our lives. Pride often stands in the way of receiving what we need to hear from God and others. One way to know if your pride is blocking God's voice is to review how often, or how little, you seek (Bible) or ask (pray) for God's guidance in your life. A humble heart that receives from God is revealed in the frequency of our seeking and asking.

Obeying What God Already Said

We all want to know what God is saying to us, but we must not overlook what he has already said. In my circle of influence I am trusted as someone who can discern the voice of God, so I regularly meet with people to sift through what they believe God might be saying to them. In listening to the many stories, one of the primary questions I ask is,

"What is the last thing God told you to do?" The answer to this question can bring confirmation or closure to their current quest for guidance.

I believe that God speaks to us daily, particularly in the context of relational dialogue in which we might hear anything from "I love you," to "Dig a little deeper into that passage." However, as we seek to hear God for directional words, we need to be careful that we are not doing so while avoiding or disregarding what he has already told us. Also, we need to be aware that the enemy will attempt to thwart our sense of direction throwing in a word of confusion which, if not detected and dealt with, can send us on a wild goose hunt.

There is a danger in constantly seeking directional words from the Lord.

There is a danger in constantly seeking directional words from the Lord. I value the prophetic ministry as much as anybody but when I talk to individuals who received 13 directional words during a conference, something is profoundly wrong. When you look at the scriptures you see how the Lord would give one prevailing directional word at a time, so that the individual could clearly obey God's voice. I am sure there are exceptions to this, but God typically speaks one thing at a time, rather than multiple directional words all at once.

Think about what God said to Noah. "Make for yourself an ark of gopher wood..." (Gen. 6:14). Following this word, God spoke to Noah in detail about what kind of boat he was to build, how big it would be, and even why he was to build it. It is estimated that Noah spent between seventy to one hundred years building the ark. What if at year thirty Noah decided to seek God for another directional word? What if Noah was tired of working on the ark, maybe a little discouraged with his progress, and wanted to know if God had anything else planned for his life? What if Noah attended the local prophetic conference and several people gave him words about starting multiple businesses and the resulting prosperity he would receive to bless thousands of people?

I think if Noah came to God and asked for another directional word, the Lord would probably say, "Noah, finish your boat." It is possible to keep ourselves from hearing God speak anything else if we do not fully obey what God has already said.

A good example of the dangers in not following through with what God already told us is found in 1 Kings 13. The Lord sends an un-named prophet to King Jeroboam in Israel to foretell the coming of a righteous king named Josiah. This news angers King Jeroboam, so he tries to have the prophet killed, but God supernaturally protects him, confirming that his word was true.

God gave specific instructions to the prophet about how he was to return home after accomplishing his mission. He said, "For so it was commanded me by the word of the Lord, saying, 'You shall eat no bread, nor drink water, nor return by the way which you came'" (1 Kgs. 13:9).

However, on his journey home, an older prophet came to him and said:

> I also am a prophet like you, and an angel spoke to me by the word of the Lord, saying, "Bring him back with you to your house, that he may eat bread and drink water." *But* he lied to him. So he went back with him, and ate bread in his house and drank water. (1 Kgs. 13:18-19)

The young prophet knew that he wasn't supposed to stop and eat while on his mission, but he allowed the supposed "word" of another prophet prevent him from obeying what God had already said. As a result of heeding the lie, the young prophet lost his life (1 Kgs. 13:20-25). While this may seem extreme, it thoroughly conveys the importance of obeying what God has already said.

I am often the last person in the prayer line ready to receive yet another prophetic word from God on top of the fifteen that I already have. Instead, I frequently pray for God to give me the grace I need to fulfill that which he has already told me to do. We must make sure that we are seeking to obey what God has already said before seeking additional direction from the Lord. It is important to be thankful for whatever God may say to us personally, rather than become addicted to the newest "word" God may have for us. God will tell us exactly what we need to know throughout the journey with him. Remember, hearing his voice is a means to achieving a goal—not the goal itself. The goal is that Christ may be formed in us and that we would fulfill all the purposes that God has in mind for each of us while on this earth.

Chapter 6 Review Questions

1. Were you able to identify any hindrances from this chapter that have effected your ability to hear from God? Which ones?

2. Have you noticed any other hindrances that are not mentioned in this chapter? If so, how would you describe them?

3. What encouraged you most about this chapter and how will you apply it to your life?

PART III

GOD'S VOICE: DISCERNING, RESPONDING, AND PURSUING

CHAPTER 7
DISCERNING GOD'S VOICE

The most common question I hear that relates to the issue of Hearing from God is, "How do I know if what I am hearing, thinking, or seeing is from God and not just myself?" This is a great question for which there are solid answers. However, as with many great questions, there are preliminary questions to which answers are first needed in order to establish a holistic perspective, whereby we may understand the most common question that we began with. In this book I have said numerous times that God speaks to everyone, but that doesn't mean that we always discern the particular moments when he speaks. Therefore, we must know and understand the process by which to determine whether something is from God or not.

We live in a world filled with noise that is blaring in our faces all the time. I would even suggest that we live in a world

A voice represents the influence of something or someone and seeks to persuade.

filled with "voices" that are constantly lobbying for our attention. In this sense, a "voice" is an expressed will, desire or opinion of something or someone seeking a response from you. A voice represents the influence of something or someone and seeks to persuade. Most people tend to think that those who hear multiple voices are crazy or somehow abnormal, which I understand can be the case. However, with this definition of a "voice," I think it's safe to say that we all hear multiple voices on a daily basis. No wonder that we have such a hard time hearing, understanding, and discerning the voice of God!

When I turned nineteen, a friend helped me get a job at a local bank. I ended up working there for a couple of years, but started as a teller making deposits, cashing checks, and counting money every day. Counterfeit money was becoming more prevalent with the emergence of high-quality printers. In response, the bank had all of the tellers go through basic training to identify counterfeit money. We were shown three ways to help determine whether a bill was real or fake. The first test for every bill was related to the paper. Real money has a specific kind of paper, and most fake bills cannot come close to the same texture. For the second test, we would take what's called a counterfeit marker and draw a short line across the bill. If the color of the line was yellow, then it was most likely a real bill, but if the line was black, then it could possibly be a counterfeit. For the final test, we learned to identify security features on the bill. The primary security feature was an embedded thread running from the top of the bill to the bottom. If the bill did not have this security feature, then it was surely a fake bill.

This process of distinguishing between a real and counterfeit bill is similar to the process of discerning the voice of God. The bank spent very little time teaching us about the details of counterfeit bills. We spent most of our time learning what an authentic bill looked and felt like so that when a counterfeit came along we could spot it quickly and not treat it as the real thing. When we seek to hear the Lord, we should already be absorbed in knowing and learning about his voice through relationship with him. Then, when another voice tries to deter us, we can identify it quickly and confidently move away from its influence.

Just as there are measures for determining authentic and counterfeit bills, so there are tests for discerning and embracing the authentic voice of God while rejecting counterfeits along the way.

When a person says, "I am trying to discern what God is saying to me," they mean that they are trying to sift through all the thoughts, feelings, fears, and other voices in order to do what they believe God is saying. To discern means to distinguish one thing from another. In the process of discovering what God is saying to us, let's remember that the goal is to know God's voice, not become experts on all the other voices swirling around us. Likewise, we should become somewhat familiar with the common voices that are not God, at least to the degree that we can identify and discard them so they won't influence our decisions and overall perspective.

In my experience with God and ministry with people, I have come to recognize several commonly-occurring voices. While my terminology may differ from yours, the character and concepts remain the same. Knowing and learning to identify these will help you as you seek to discern the voice of God in your life.

The Voice of the Enemy

When it comes to the voice of the enemy there are several things we need to understand. First, the devil is not equal to God in any way. While he does have some power, he is limited as a created being and in no way exhibits the same attributes that God possesses. For example, the devil is not omnipresent like God. God's presence can be everywhere at the same time, but the devil can only be one place at one time. This should seem obvious, but the way that some reference the activities of the devil, you get the sense that he may be omnipresent.

When we talk about the voice of the enemy, we are not referencing the devil only. The devil works with and among a demonic cohort involved in opposing the work of God in humankind (Eph. 6:12). Additionally, the devil is the leader, planner, and mastermind behind the demonic voices that we will come in contact with from time to time (Eph. 6:11). While we don't want to give the devil and demonic spirits too much credit, we should not be ignorant of their plan to direct us away from God's voice.

The Apostle Paul clearly recognized that the devil had a plan against what he was doing for God (2 Cor. 2:11). The same is true for us. The truth is that God has a plan *for* your life and the enemy has a plan *against* your life. There are times when people have said to me, "I have never experienced spiritual warfare or heard the voice of the enemy." If that is true, it is prob-

> **The truth is that God has a plan *for* your life and the enemy has a plan *against* your life.**

ably because the enemy doesn't see you as a threat, or you are not fully aware of how he seeks to come against you. In scripture one of the primary ways that the enemy attacks the people of God is by distorting what God has said (e.g., Gen. 3:1-5; Matt. 4:1-11).

There are two primary ways that we will encounter the voice of the enemy. The first is through our thoughts. The enemy will transmit thoughts into our minds in order to distract, convince, or deceive us. This goes back to what we discussed in chapter four—not all of our thoughts originate from within. These thoughts can range from statements like, "Just compromise a little bit, nobody will know," to "Kill yourself." For example, the enemy will attempt to sow thoughts into our minds in order to convince us that these are our own thoughts. When we believe the enemy's lies, the very enemy of God is successfully influencing us. We need discernment and God's truth to identify the lies and stand against the enemy!

The second primary way that we will encounter the voice of the enemy is through the physical voices of other people. Sometimes, a person will say or do something to us that is demonically inspired. The Apostle Paul refers to the influence of the enemy behind the actions of those who were persecuting him when writing to the Ephesian church.

> For our struggle is not against flesh and blood, but against
> the rulers, against the powers, against the world forces of this

darkness, against the spiritual *forces* of wickedness in the heavenly *places*. (Eph. 6:12)

I am not suggesting a person has to be possessed to speak a demonic thought, but they may be totally undiscerning about the origin of their words, and ignorantly become a vessel for the enemy. Often, the voice of the enemy will come in both ways at the same time. The sowing of thoughts into our minds is a direct attack, and the words of an undiscerning person is an indirect attack. The direct attack is like planting seeds into our minds, while the indirect attack waters those seeds.

When I was young I was regularly asked, "What's wrong with you?" I was typically straight-faced, and plenty of people interpreted this to mean I was angry or sad. Usually, I was neither, but because we judge mostly by what we see, many assumed this about me, which caused me to feel extremely misunderstood. As I got older, I continued to hear comments about my non-emotional facial expressions, which earned me a reputation of being a jerk. Even as a young Christian I started hearing these words in my mind, "You're a jerk," or, "You don't care about people," and, "You're not loving."

What started as questions from others became bombarding thoughts from the enemy on a regular basis. When I became a pastor, I started comparing myself to other men of God who seemed really loving. If the combination of the enemy's thoughts and my own insecurities wasn't enough, I started hearing reports of people saying similar things about me as well. "I am not loving and shouldn't be a pastor," I thought. With others speaking the enemy's accusations over me, I totally bought into it.

One day I was at a friend's house helping him remodel his bathroom, and while on my knees installing his floor something marvelous happened to me. In that moment, I was overwhelmed with the same old thoughts, "You're not loving like pastor so and so...." As this was happening, I heard the Lord ask me a question: "What is love, Ben?" I thought about this for a moment, and then it hit me! Love was not about mere words or facial expressions. Love was about considering others better than yourself in what you say and *do*. "I am a loving person, that's why I am here helping my friend remodel his bathroom," I said out loud! As I spoke, it was like the Lord just smiled at me and winked.

The combination of the enemy's lies and the voice of others had formed a false perspective about my identity, which I totally owned. The horrible part was that it was all a lie. When the Lord asked me a question about love, he broke the power of the enemy's lie and imparted a new discernment that has since protected me from such deception. If you have bought into the lies of the enemy, I sure hope you kept the receipt because you are going to have to take them back!

If you have bought into the lies of the enemy, I sure hope you kept the receipt because you are going to have to take them back!

The voice of an individual always represents his or her character. Likewise, God's voice will always be in line with his character, and the enemy's voice will flow from his character. The Bible reveals the nature of our enemy, so we will need to know what it says about him in order to better discern his voice and avoid his influence.

In Revelation 12:9-10 we read that the devil is an accuser. In Genesis 3, he tempts Adam and Eve to disobey God, as he does Jesus in Matthew 4. If you read both accounts you will not only find that the devil is a tempter, but he also tries to skew God's word so the one being tempted will compromise and believe less than what God has said. The devil is a liar and the father of lies (John 8:44). The devil is a sinner and a promoter of sin to all who will listen to his voice (1 John 3:8). This is the character of the devil and this is what his voice sounds like: accusation, condemnation, lies, falsehood, temptation, hatred, disobedience, lust, pride, and the like.

Remember, the enemy cannot force us to do anything, so he uses deception and trickery to manipulate us. This means that we will not always easily detect his lies coming against us. For some reason, most people have this idea that the devil is a horned evil creature that is so nasty we should easily be able to discern his works and words. However, the Bible tells us that the enemy reveals himself differently from what the movies suggest: "No wonder, for even Satan disguises himself as an angel of light" (2 Cor. 11:14).

Jesus has defeated the devil and his demonic forces through his death, burial, and resurrection. As Christians, we stand in the victory of Jesus Christ and should never fear the devil or demons. However, we should be aware that our enemy, although defeated, will still seek an opportunity to destroy us if we allow it. The Apostle Peter exhorted us to be aware of the enemy in such a way that we could resist him. May we be able to discern the enemy's activity in order to avoid his influence entirely as we pursue the voice of the Lord.

> Be of sober *spirit,* be on the alert. Your adversary, the devil, prowls around like a roaring lion, seeking someone to devour. But resist him, firm in *your* faith, knowing that the same experiences of suffering are being accomplished by your brethren who are in the world. (1 Pet. 5:8-9)

The Voice of the Flesh

You are probably aware that even if you have given your whole life to God, there is a part of you that still wants to rebel and act selfishly. Before we became Christians, our self-centeredness ran rampant, in search of unending personal gratification. As Christians, we are now born again, filled with the Spirit, and able to put to death our old selfish ways that once controlled us. Our flesh remains infected with the same sinful appetite that once dominated our lives. Although it no longer dominates us, this appetite definitely calls aloud to us daily.

The Apostle Paul wrote at great length on the appetite of the flesh. In the majority of his letters you will find some kind of exhortation to the churches to "walk in the Spirit" and not in the flesh (Gal. 5:16). In other words, we ought to walk under the influence, or voice, of the

Spirit rather than of the flesh in everything we think, say, and do. God has called us out of a life of listening to our own voices and into a life of listening to his voice. The voice of the flesh will constantly seek to influence us by putting our own interests before God's and others'.

God has called us out of a life of listening to our own voices and into a life of listening to his voice.

It is my opinion that a large number of Christians don't discern the voice of the flesh and consequently are living under its influence without even realizing it. As Christians we are called to grow through the renewing of our minds (Rom. 12:1-2), which can only happen through a consistent relationship with the Lord through studying his word and daily prayer. Without intentionally choosing to be daily influenced by God's voice, we will default to listening to our own voices without realizing it. If you have a tendency to neglect spending time with God, then let me provoke you by saying that, in order for you to discern God's voice in your life, this will need to change.

Please understand, all of us are in the battle against our flesh and for God's Spirit to be in control (Gal. 5:17). However, we can only win the battle and overcome the flesh if we fully yield to the power of the Holy Spirit. This does not happen without investing daily in relationship with God, trusting him for what we cannot do.

I think the voice of the flesh is best represented by Jesus' parable from Luke 8. Jesus said that his kingdom was like a man who sowed seed which fell on four different types of soil. The four kinds of soil represent four different kinds of hearts. Some of the seeds fell among thorns, which would eventually choke the seed and make it unfruitful. Jesus explains this particular soil in this way.

> The *seed* which fell among the thorns, these are the ones
> who have heard, and as they go on their way they are choked

with worries and riches and pleasures of *this* life, and bring no fruit to maturity. (Luke 8:14)

The worries, riches, and pleasures of this life are at the core of the voice of the flesh. Jesus told us in this passage that the power of this voice is so great that it will choke out his voice (seed) if we allow it. We must learn to discern the voice of the flesh and pull down selfishness in our lives; otherwise, we cannot please God (Rom. 8:5-8).

The Voice of Our Past

You may remember the story when, during a baseball game, I was hit with a bat in the side of the head, causing permanent damage to my right ear. This event from my past has hindered my physical ability to hear well in the present. I think the same can be true spiritually. The difficult and tragic events of the past can impact us so dramatically that we have a hard time hearing God's voice today. Maybe your past is riddled with all kinds of terrible things that you have done or things that have been done against you. You will need to be aware that such experiences can hinder you from hearing and moving forward with God.

Jesus said to those that would follow him, "No one, after putting his hand to the plow and looking back, is fit for the kingdom of God" (Luke 9:62). There will always be a temptation to look back rather than pay attention to the invitation of Jesus right here and right now. The enemy will try to use the voices of our past to keep us living insignificant lives.

> **The enemy will try to use the voices of our past to keep us living insignificant lives.**

We are called to do significant things, not because of what we have or have not done, but because of what Jesus has done. When we give our lives to the Lord and repent of our old lives, we become new in every way. "Therefore if anyone is in Christ, *he is* a new creature; the old things passed away; behold, new things have come" (2 Cor. 5:17). We have been forgiven and cleansed from those old things, and the Bible says that God doesn't remember our sins anymore (Heb. 10:16-18).

Moses was a murderer, Abraham a liar, Peter a coward, Paul a murderer, and Matthew an extortionist. It pleased God to use those whose pasts were riddled with things opposite of what God asked them to do. The voice of the past will try to remind us of what we were and what we did. Whenever God speaks to you and the enemy suddenly tries to disqualify you by reminding you of what you have done, just remind him and yourself of what Jesus has done and move on with the stuff of God's kingdom.

The Voice of the World

While we are clearly called to love the *people* of the world as Jesus does (John 3:16), we are also called to abstain from loving the *things* in the world.

> Do not love the world or the things in the world. If anyone loves the world, the love of the Father is not in him. For all that is in the world, the lust of the flesh and the lust of the eyes and the boastful pride of life, is not from the Father, but is from the world. The world is passing away, and *also* its lusts; but the one who does the will of God lives forever. (1 John 2:15-17)

The voice of the world is the collective non-Christian perspective that is promoted by any widespread cultural mediums such as music, movies, Internet, radio, books, politics, etc. The only kingdom that is one hundred percent honoring to the name and purposes of Jesus is the Kingdom of God. Every other kingdom will fall short and compromise the sovereign will, purposes, and perspectives of King Jesus.

The Bible calls us to remain unstained by the world (Jas. 1:27), and to be in it but not of it (John 17:13-19). We also know that the devil is the ruler of *this* world (2 Cor. 4:4). What does all this mean? It means that the primary influence of the surrounding world will promote the flesh and rebellion to a holy God. This voice will not always be clear so it will require discernment to detect its influence.

One day I was driving on the freeway from Los Angeles to Hollywood. Not being from California, I paid special attention to all the billboard advertisements. I counted two billboards dedicated to strip clubs and at least three promoting some kind of alcoholic beverage. I am sure most people who drive by these every day think nothing of them, but it grieved me to see them.

The strip-club billboards had no sexual graphics or outright sexual language, but rather advertised a discreet "gentleman's club" in such a way that you might think it was an acceptable, almost classy place for men to go and have a good time. A great place, right? A wonderful place for true *gentlemen*, right? Not a place where husbands go and cheat on their wives, or where women sell themselves and allow their bodies to define their value? Not a place where young men learn a false sexual intimacy, only to bring that into their marriage bedrooms, confusing their wives, right?

The voice of the world seeks to cover the truth. A strip club is a gentleman's hangout. A fifth of hard liquor is a Lamborghini™ and two good-looking people out on the town. Really, nobody believes that a strip club is a great place for the whole family and nobody believes if they drink a fifth of vodka and smoke cigarettes they will look like the people on the billboard. What we are missing from these pictures is the truth!

The voice of the world is telling us what to think and seeking to redefine the truth by covering it with lies. I am shocked that most Christians will listen to music, indiscriminately, that clearly glorifies sins that Jesus gave his life to eradicate from our lives. Music is a voice. Media is a voice. What we watch, listen to, and read will either influence us with truth or influence us with lies. A person who claims to not be influenced by such things is already not discerning the voice of the world from the voice of God.

If we are going to discern the voice of the Lord from the voice of the world we will need to be radical in our approach to the things of the world. The last I read, the average American watches two to three hours of television per day. Compare that to the latest statistic that most American evangelical Christians read their Bibles once a week on average. This should convict us. How can we discern the Lord's voice from the world's voice when our time is given to everything but God? The answer is simple—we can't. If you have an overage of media in your life, I strongly urge you to fast from it for a time and in some cases entirely, depending on the content. Many people that I encourage to create more room for God's voice report that they begin hearing him like never before.

In our culture, the voice of the world is extremely loud and the only way for the volume to decrease is to literally do something about it.

In our culture, the voice of the world is extremely loud and the only way for the volume to decrease is to literally do something about it. We must make it a habit to turn off our televisions, turn off our stereos in the car, and put down our smart phones. God's voice, which has been there all along, will come across loudly and clearly as we intentionally turn down the voice of the world.

The Voice of the Crowd

Have you ever been with a group of people that all wanted to do the same thing while you were the only one who didn't? While ministering in prison, I can't tell you how many stories I heard of individuals who got into a car with the wrong people at the wrong time and it changed their lives for the worse. There is a group pressure, unlike anything else, that promotes doing and saying certain things. Unless you are a strong person and willing to be ridiculed or worse, you probably get pushed into doing things you don't want to do. That's what I call listening to the voice of the crowd.

The voice of the crowd is the "majority-rules" model that has power to persuade others within the crowd, whether they like it or not. In the Bible, as the crowd gathers during the sentencing of Jesus, they collectively urged Pilate to crucify Jesus.

> But Pilate said to them, "Why, what evil has He done?" *But they shouted all the more*, "Crucify Him!" Wishing to satisfy the *crowd*, Pilate released Barabbas for them, and after having Jesus scourged, he handed Him over to be crucified. (Mark 15:14-15)

It is clear from the gospel accounts that Pilate did not understand why the Jews wanted Jesus dead, but the voice of the crowd was so strong that he gave into the pressure and had Jesus crucified.

Several times in the book of Acts we see the crowds being stirred up against those who preached the gospel. There were always groups in various cities that would incite the crowd against Paul and his companions (Acts 14:19; 16:22; 17:13; 21:27). I am sure there were plenty of people in these crowds that either opposed what was being said or had no opinion, but because they were afraid to stand against the crowd, the pressure caused them to become another voice from within it.

The Lord will often speak to us about something that goes against the grain of what everybody else thinks or says.

The Lord will often speak to us about something that goes against the grain of what everybody else thinks or says. If we push down God's voice and allow the pressures of the collective voice around us to overrule God, we will grow dull to his voice and struggle to discern what he is saying. We must not allow the voice of the crowd to pressure us into being another yes-man to what everybody wants. If we know something isn't right we need to speak up, which will result in increased discernment of the Lord's voice.

The Voice of the Lord

As I said earlier, our goal is not to become experts on all the other voices around us, but rather to become extremely familiar with the voice of the Lord in our daily lives. God's voice will always be in line with his character, which we can discover clearly through scripture. God's voice will be like a Good Father (Matt. 7:11), extremely loving (1 John 4:16), and no matter what he says it will be for our good (Rom. 8:28-29).

While this should go without saying, we must remember who is following whom. To correctly discern the voice of the Lord we are not looking for what makes us feel good or what sounds the closest to what we want. Jesus said, "My sheep hear my voice, and I know them, and they follow me" (John 10:27). As followers of Jesus we are called to both hear and follow him. I think a lot of people get tripped up because they are looking for something instead of *someone*. When I talk with the Lord about direction I will often say, "Lord, please speak to me, and no matter what you say, I will follow." Maybe I don't need to tell the Lord something he knows better than I do, but a personal reminder helps me remember that I am looking for what he wants and not what I want.

To know the voice of the Lord is to know the Lord, through which we are able to identify all the other voices well enough to discard the counterfeits. If you believe God is speaking to you but you are unsure as to whether or not it is him, I encourage you to review and apply the next section on "The Process for Discerning God's Voice." I apply this process in my own life and believe it will help you with your journey as well.

The Process for Discerning God's Voice

The Scripture Test

While not everything that God will say to us will be in the form of a Bible verse, we must know that it will *never* contradict the written word of God. The Bible is the general will of God for all people in all generations and it does not change. We must always *first* submit what we believe God is saying to the scripture test. Does the word (vision, dream, thought, etc) adhere to scriptural principles? Does anything about the word you received contradict what God has revealed in the Bible? Is there anything about the word you received that is suspect when you analyze it alongside sound Bible teaching?

If what you believe God is saying does not make it past this test, you may simply discard it. If what you believe God has said to you doesn't contradict the Bible, then you just continue with the discernment process.

Ask Good Questions

By asking good questions, we effectively probe our hearts and minds to see if what we think God has said is really God or something we just want. For example, some good questions are, "Do I have peace about this word—why or why not?" Also, "Is this word in line with other things that God has been saying?" If something is not even close to other things God has said to you, you will want to be more cautious, particularly with a directional type of word.

I even ask myself simple questions like, "Why do I think this is God?" Having to articulate these things will help us further discern whether something is from God or not. When people come to me and I begin asking them such questions, they sometimes become uncomfortable, which can be a sign that it may not be God. When all we want is to follow the voice of God, we should welcome the probing of our hearts with various questions.

Commit the Word to Prayer

When God speaks to me and I am trying to discern whether it's all from Him, partially from him, or otherwise, I begin praying about it right away. In prayer I ask the Lord to reveal if he is speaking to me. I patiently wait on his gentle voice of confirmation. I have been guilty of thinking what God was telling me was meant for next month when it really was meant for ten years later. When God confirms something to you, unless he speaks directly to you about the timing, don't assume you know. Knowing this, I patiently pray about things and ask God to impart the appropriate level of urgency so I can obey Him properly.

Seek Godly Counsel

In Proverbs 15:22 we read, "Without consultation, plans are frustrated, but with many counselors they succeed." The idea behind this passage is that we often need help to determine if what we are thinking is actually right. In the case of discerning God's voice, I can't stress enough the importance of involving trustworthy voices in our process. When we bring others into the discernment process we are asking them to discern with us, but not to tell us if it is from God or not. After sharing what I am hearing, I usually ask the trusted people in my life to pray about it and respond in somewhat of a timely manner. God has used people in my life to help me see when he is speaking to me and also when he is not.

This step is especially important when we are just learning to hear God's voice. When you read the story of Samuel you can see very clearly how God used the Priest Eli to help Samuel see that God was actually talking to him (1 Sam. 3:1-14). Samuel did not know the voice of the Lord at all so he needed help, just like we do as we begin to grow in hearing God's voice.

Ask for Confirmation

When we believe God is speaking to us about something important, I believe it's okay to ask for confirmation of some kind. At times, the Lord will bring confirmation through our personal prayer time, a prophetic word, or even a casual conversation with a friend. The way in which we receive confirmation will vary, but our heavenly Father loves us enough to ensure that we are truly hearing him.

It is important to remember that God wants us to hear him more than we do. If that is true, then confirming something is no big deal, especially when the word or sense from God has a level of obscurity attached to it. If I were in a conversation with my son and, for whatever reason, he missed a piece of what I said, I would be glad to repeat the whole conversation if my son sincerely asked me to say it again. In your discernment process, just look to the Lord and say, "Father, please give me clarity in what you are saying so I can follow you with all my heart." I guarantee that your sincere request will always be met with confirmation at some point from your heavenly Father!

It is important to remember that God wants us to hear him more than we do.

Chapter 7 Review Questions

1. Have you been able to identify any counterfeit voices in your life? How will you deal with them?

2. What parts of the "Process for Discerning God's Voice" are you already using? What parts were you not using that you intend to use?

3. What encouraged you most about this chapter and how will you apply it to your life?

CHAPTER 8
RESPONDING TO GOD'S VOICE

While hearing God is truly a privilege, it also brings with it great responsibility. The fact is, if we don't want to *respond* to what God says, than we shouldn't want to *hear* what he says either! What we do with what God says is incredibly important. I want to stress this point because my hope is that we would never become casual with anything that God says to us. The majority of what we will hear from God requires a response, so we need to be prepared to act.

The majority of what we will hear from God requires a response, so we need to be prepared to act.

The most widely-known sermon that Jesus ever preached is in Matthew, chapters five through seven. This sermon is commonly referred to as "The Sermon on the Mount," during which Jesus went up the mountainside and began teaching the crowds about life in the Kingdom of God. His teaching made kingdom-living accessible to every person—not just the spiritually elite. This kind of teaching was revolutionary in itself, but in addition, all who heard and responded to Jesus were on equal ground, which was previously unheard of. For our purposes, the most important part of his sermon occurs at the very end and deals exclusively with what everyone present should do with what they just heard Jesus say.

> Therefore everyone who hears these words of Mine and acts on them, may be compared to a wise man who built his house on the rock. And the rain fell, and the floods came, and the winds blew and slammed against that house; and *yet* it did not fall, for it had been founded on the rock. Everyone who hears these words of Mine and does not act on them, will be like a foolish man who built his house on the sand. The rain fell, and the floods came, and the winds blew and slammed against that house; and it fell—and great was its fall. (Matt.7:24-27)

Jesus makes it extremely clear that the person who hears his words and does not act on them is foolish and can expect a definite collapse in life. Therefore, hearing from God, whether we are reading the Bible or discerning the voice of the Holy Spirit, must be accompanied by a commitment to respond. What we do with what he says defines who we are and profoundly effects our future.

One Sunday evening while in attendance at a small church, I had my first encounter with an international missionary. He was from India and traveled to the United States once a year to raise support and recruit people to become missionaries in the remote parts of his country. His stories were compelling and sounded similar to what I read in the Bible about people like Abraham, Elijah, and Daniel. The more stories that he told the more I was both challenged and discouraged. I was discouraged because my life seemed so far from the things that God was doing in and through him and I didn't see that changing unless I moved to India or something similar. In some ways I think many young Christians feel like this at some point, but God ultimately clarifies that it's not about where you are but how you choose to live where ever you are. This missionary was just a man who both heard *and* responded to what God said to him, and as a result was able to see and share of God's great love and mighty power with a vast number of people.

God's plan for this world is not only decided but will also truly come to pass. Somehow, that truth has caused many people to think or teach that our responsibility is not that important because they think that God is the one that does it all. Really? God does it all? He hasn't invited us to participate in the unfolding of his will? He doesn't place any responsibility on us to do anything? Obviously, this view becomes confusing when you start challenging it with the implications of countless Bible verses. But if we don't discuss this to some degree, the issue of responding to God's voice won't make much sense.

First, let's be clear. God can do everything without us and has done most things without any of us. However, throughout the Bible we can clearly see how God desires to use people to accomplish his will. While I believe that God is sovereign, I also believe that, in his sovereignty, he allows us to make choices. We can choose to obey or not. God desires for us to work with him to accomplish his purposes; I think that this was a more difficult approach for him to take. Sometimes my kids want to help me paint a bedroom or clean the garage, and when I allow them to do so they usually make more of a mess for mom and dad to clean up. However, the experiences that we share during these times typically prove helpful for teaching and building relationships, which really is the point. We are not only recipients of God's plan but we also become co-laborers in it (1 Cor. 3:9), making our response to his voice all the more important.

There is more to the plan of God than we might suppose, especially because his plan has a lot to do with us. We are God's tools through whom he continues the message and ministry of Jesus Christ. Hearing God's voice is not only important; it's essential as we engage the missional aspect of walking with God so that the whole world can be awakened to his reality.

I continue to encounter many Christians who, for whatever reasons, don't seem to think that their roles in what God is doing matters that much. What a lie. You matter. What you do matters. What you choose not to do matters. How many people are waiting on the other side of our response to God's voice? How many wrong things will be made right when we

How many wrong things will be right when we choose to follow God's leadership and not our own?

choose to follow God's leadership and not our own? It's time to shake off the false notions that our responses or our choices don't matter much, while embracing the awesome privilege of serving God and seeing lives changed through his power as we respond to his voice.

One summer I was invited to speak at an outdoor festival in a park just about an hour or so from where I live. We arrived and I preached my message, then my friends and I began walking to our cars and while crossing the street I walked past two young men that worked for Parks and Recreation. The Holy Spirit spoke to me, "Turn around and go talk to them!" I took a few more steps, turned around and walked up to them. As we began some small talk, the Holy Spirit spoke to my heart about one of their sisters who had recently almost died from a drug overdose. I shared this word with the young man. With tears in his eyes he acknowledged the truth of this and recalled the details of how his sister had almost died. He and the other young man were not Christians but I boldly encouraged them in the Lord and asked if I could pray for them. As they nodded "yes" to prayer, they both took off their hats as I began to pray for his sister and family. I finished praying and began sharing about God's love in Jesus Christ and how I had come to know this love at nineteen years old.

Neither of the young guys gave their lives to Jesus that day but, without a doubt, that was probably the most eye-opening experience they had ever witnessed. I wouldn't be surprised if both of them were walking with Jesus today—that is just how God works, one step at a time. This testimony is the result of hearing *and* responding to the voice of God. What would have happened if I kept walking? That's right—nothing. This is the kind of stuff that happens every day when people hear the voice of God and, instead of sitting by passively, they respond to what they hear. How many testimonies of God's goodness toward people are we holding back because we're not listening, or listening but not responding? It's time to rise up friends—it's time.

The Heart That Responds

One day I was reading the story of when Jesus walked up to a man named Matthew and simply said, "Follow me!" (Matt. 9:9) Matthew was a tax collector in the city of Capernaum, and when Jesus called him he was in the process of collecting taxes. The fascinating part of this story is how Matthew responds: "And he got up and followed Him" (Matt. 9:9). Seriously? Can you imagine that for a moment? Matthew got up, left his job, and began walking with Jesus for the next several years because of two simple words. If that is not a radical response, then I don't know what is.

I asked the Lord, "Why did you choose the men that you did to be your disciples?" Within seconds, the Lord spoke to my heart, "I chose them because they were humble." Immediately, I thought of when Jesus referred to himself as "humble in heart" (Matt. 11:29). Responding to God is all about having a humble heart, just like Jesus demonstrated.

Having a humble heart is the key to properly responding to God. For example, look at the difference between Moses and Pharaoh. Moses was called by God and, although his response was not perfect, he obeyed God's leading. The Bible also says that Moses was more humble than any other man (Num. 12:3). Pharaoh was told what God wanted and he refused to listen because his heart was hard (Exod. 7:14). These different responses reveal the condition of both men's hearts. I think the same is true for us; the ways we respond (or don't respond) to God demonstrates the measure of heart-humility we each possess.

Isn't it interesting that Jesus chose to compare his followers to sheep, which are widely known for being humble and for instinctively following their shepherd? His sheep hear his voice *and* follow (John 10:27). As Christians, we too should approach hearing from God and responding to what he says with the same humility. If we struggle with believing or obeying God, then we should examine the condition of our hearts.

If we struggle with believing or obeying God, then we should examine the condition of our hearts.

I'd like to encourage you with a prayer that King David prayed for his son Solomon, which I pray over my family and myself regularly. "[G]ive to my son Solomon a perfect heart to keep Your commandments..." (1 Chron. 29:19). God doesn't expect us to accomplish things without empowering us to do so, which is why we must ask him for obedient hearts so that we are ready to do what we hear him say.

Responding with Faith

Our first and most important response to God's voice is the response of faith. Now before you check out and assume you know what I mean, let's explore this topic a bit. First of all, what is faith? Faith is assurance, trust, belief, and conviction. Faith is our ability to believe and trust that something is true beyond what we *know* and beyond what we can *see*. Where do you get faith? We know that faith comes from God because the Bible says that God has given each person a measure of faith (Rom.12:3). While every person has faith, the real question is what should we apply our faith to? Some people put their faith in themselves, a system, the words of others, or maybe in nothing at all. God gives us faith so that when we hear his voice we can apply it toward whatever he says. Do we believe and trust in what God says, or do we believe something else?

Over and over we read in the Bible about God speaking to someone and fully expecting that person to believe him regardless of the circumstance. Having faith in something isn't about optimism, what we want, or what we think should happen, or even what we can see. It's all about believing, trusting, and relying fully upon what God says. Therefore, knowing what God is saying to us is only the beginning! After we know what God has said, it comes down to what we believe, to what we choose to put our faith in.

The writer of Hebrews went to great lengths to help us understand the power of responding by faith in our relationship with God. "Now faith is the assurance of *things* hoped for, the conviction of things not seen. For by it the men of old gained approval" (Heb. 11:1-2). When you read through Hebrews 11 you get a quick glimpse of several people who heard God in their day and believed him even when their lives were on the line. Men like Noah, Abraham, Joseph, and Moses heard God's voice and responded by faith. In many cases in the Bible, the only thing these and other heroes of faith had was a word from God.

Let me illustrate the response of faith. In the beginning of 2013 I decided to lose some weight because, well, let's just say I needed to. After many conversations with various people, each of whom thought their particular method of losing weight was fool-proof, a friend of mine convinced me that I needed to count calories, and that if I held to the program I would surely lose weight. So I did it. I believed what my friend told me, but that belief required action in order to produce results. So, I followed the program exactly as he explained it to me, and over a period of several months I lost almost fifteen pounds and have since kept it off.

I believed what I was told and consequently oriented my life around what my friend said. My faith (using that term loosely here) caused me to believe resulting in action. Faith toward God's word is similar in that it's not just a mental acknowledgement; true faith trusts what he says unto action. In other words, faith carries obedience with it; otherwise, it's not real faith (Jas. 2:17). The men of old gained approval through faith because, through their actions, their faith was made known to the world in which they lived. Having faith in what God says requires a certain attitude and is always accompanied by specific actions.

At this point I need to warn you that if you truly hear God and respond to him by faith, some people might just think that you're crazy. Think about those who are mentioned in Hebrews 11, like Noah for example (Heb. 11:7). God told Noah to build a huge boat because he was about to judge the whole world with a massive flood. Noah believed God and started working on the boat project for the next seventy to one hundred years. What do you think his neighbors thought about his building of this boat? Can you imagine Noah explaining why he was building a boat? Can you see their faces? I am sure the whole town thought that Noah was crazy, at least until the flood came.

Hearing from God is about changing the world, but the world isn't changed unless people who hear God place their faith in what he says. Hebrews 11 gives incredible en-

Hearing from God is about changing the world, but the world isn't changed unless people who hear God place their faith in what he says.

couragement to those who will believe God. "By faith we understand that the worlds were prepared by the word of God, so that what is seen was not made out of things which are visible" (Heb. 11:3). I once believed that this verse meant that it takes faith to believe that God made the universe, but that's not at all what it means. Remember, the context for this verse and chapter is a long list of people who heard God, placed their faith in his word, and changed the world as a result.

When you look at verse three, notice the word "worlds." The original word behind "worlds" is often translated ages, eras, periods of time, and generations.[14] This word always speaks of a period of time, not a physical world or universe. Restated, this verse really means that God framed the past generations through a partnership with those who would believe and apply their faith to what he said to them. The author wants us to understand how serious the issue of faith really is. Our role in changing the world begins with hearing God and continues with an unwavering commitment to place our faith in what he says.

Responding with Obedience

What comes to mind when someone talks about "obeying God?" I run across a number of people who tend to hear, "you'd *better* obey God" rather than, "we get to obey God." Everything about God is an invitation, not an obligation, even when it comes to the issue of obedience. We should want to obey God because we believe him, trust him, and love him, not to mention the fact that he is God and knows our past, present, and future.

God wants us to obey him because he knows what's best for us. The blessed life is always the obedient life. In a healthy family, when a child disobeys, it usually stems from selfishness and pride. The disobedient child either doesn't want to do something that they should do (even though they know it's good for them), or they don't want to do something because they believe they know better. Both reasons are utterly foolish.

A common example is when a father tell his son to brush his teeth. "Okay dad, I will make sure to brush my teeth before I go to bed." Does the son do it? Usually not. "Make sure you floss your teeth as well, because if you don't floss you will get cavities!" "Sure dad, I will take care of it because that is really on my priority list." The child can go quite a while without any consequences, which probably empowers his disobedience all the more. "I don't need to floss, my teeth are fine. Dad doesn't know what he's talking about." A year later the child is in the dentist's chair hearing the bad news: "You have four cavities and we will be doing the fillings today." Now, all of a sudden, this son hears his dad's words in a new light as the numbing needle is shoved into his mouth. Hopefully in this moment he realizes that the pain, discomfort, and inconvenience he is experiencing is the consequence of his disobedience.

Good parents don't tell their kids what to do because they somehow enjoy controlling them or making them do needless things that don't matter. Parents tell their kids what to do and desire an obedient response because it's in the child's best interest. The kids need to trust the parents in order to believe them and obey what they are told to do. Obviously, trusting the parents' character is the key.

We are God's kids and the Lord wants us to trust him to the point at which our obedience becomes the natural outflow of our rela-

> **Parents tell their kids what to do and desire an obedient response because it's in the child's best interest.**

tionship with Him. On the night of Jesus' betrayal he shared some very important and intimate words with his disciples, much of which would require a response after he was gone. Knowing this, he said, "If you love Me, you will keep My commandments" (John 14:15). Jesus shared his heart for his disciples by saying that the most important thing that they could do while he was gone would be to obey all the things he told them. You can almost hear Jesus saying, "Hey guys, if you really love me and want to know what I want for you, just remember all the things I told you and do them, because it's not only what I want for you, it's what's best for you."

When it comes to responding in obedience you simply can't overlook the story of Abraham. We are briefly introduced to Abram (i.e., Abraham) at the end of Genesis 11 and really get a glimpse of his faith in God at the beginning of chapter 12.

> Now the LORD said to Abram, "*Go forth* from your country, And from your relatives And from your father's house, To the land which I will show you; And I will make you a great nation, And I will bless you, And make your name great; And so you shall be a blessing; And I will bless those who bless

you. And the one who curses you I will curse. And in you all
the families of the earth will be blessed." So Abram went forth
as the LORD had spoken to him; and Lot went with him.
Now Abram was seventy-five years old when he departed from
Haran. (Gen. 12:1-4)

God spoke to Abraham about leaving his country and going to
a new and unfamiliar land. Most people read this passage and focus
on the promises given instead of the response necessary to fulfill the
promises. If Abraham did not *go*, would God still have blessed him
and fulfilled the promises he gave him? I don't think so. Was Abraham's
obedience important? Absolutely! The Bible is full of promises that
require a response of obedience. From this passage we see literally that
the obedient life is the blessed life. What incredible things await us, our
families, churches, and cities on the other side of our obedience!

When it comes to hearing the voice of God there are two kinds of
obedience. The first kind is what I call *immediate obedience*, in which
God speaks to us and our obedience is required and contained within
that moment. If we choose not to obey God immediately, the opportunity is lost and any potential fruit is forfeited.

Not long ago, I was on my way to a meeting, in a hurry as usual, so
I pulled up to the drive-through of the closest fast-food place I could
find. I ordered my food and pulled up to the window when suddenly,
the Lord spoke to me (internal voice) about the employee in the drive-
through. I heard the Lord say, "He is supposed to go back to college and
pursue a career in writing and I want you to encourage him to pray to
me and trust that I can help him with the money that he needs." When
I pulled up to receive my meal, the man took my money and right then
I shared with him exactly what I believed the Lord had told me. He
said, "Are you kidding me? I was just talking to my brother today about
going back to school to be a journalist—this is crazy!" I briefly shared
with him the love of God in Jesus Christ and encouraged him to pray.
He was both freaked out and encouraged at the same time. What an
incredible moment that was for this young man. I literally had seconds

to obey what I heard the Lord say. This kind of opportunity requires us to obey the Lord immediately or the opportunity is lost. I am sure that this young man was glad that I obeyed.

The second kind of obedience is what I call *long-term obedience*, in which God speaks to you about something that will require ongoing effort to carry out his word to you. God told Noah to build a boat that took about 70 to 100 years to complete. God told Abraham to go to a foreign land, which may have taken months or years. The Bible is full of examples wherein people were required to live in continued long-term obedience to what God said. When God speaks to you about something that requires long-term obedience, it will always be accompanied with continued faith and real perseverance.

I personally receive many words from the Lord that require immediate obedience and very few requiring long-term obedience. This is true for all of us. Words that require long-term obedience are mostly directional and can involve months and years, which explains why we receive fewer of them. God may give us daily words that require immediate obedience for the purpose of sharing the gospel or bringing encouragement. Regardless of what God asks us to do, long- or short-term, we can trust that he will empower us to obey his voice in all things. As a result, the world, our world, will be changed.

Responding with Courage

If we are going to respond to what God says we will need to be people of courage, willing to face difficulty and take risks, and not allowing the fear of what might happen or what others might say to stop us from doing the will of God. God calls people to do great things; as such, risks are always involved, which is why courage is so necessary.

Before Moses died he commissioned a successor, Joshua, to lead the people of Israel into the Promised Land. Moses was 120 years old and he knew that he would not lead the people into the land, so it was time for a change of leadership before he died. Moses laid his hands on Joshua to commission him into his new leadership role and spoke these words to him:

Then He commissioned Joshua the son of Nun, and said,
"Be strong and courageous, for you shall bring the sons of
Israel into the land which I swore to them, and I will be with
you." (Deut. 31:23)

The call of God that was on Moses was being transferred to Joshua,
and if anyone knew what it would take to follow the will of God and
lead the people of Israel it was Moses. What does Moses tell Joshua?
"Be strong and courageous!" Not long after this commissioning prayer,
Moses dies and the Lord begins speaking to Joshua with the same
words that Moses had given him.

Have I not commanded you? Be strong and courageous!
Do not tremble or be dismayed, for the LORD your God is
with you wherever you go. (Josh. 1:9)

God told Joshua to have courage because he was about to face huge
obstacles in his new role. Over the next several years Joshua would go
on to lead more than thirty military campaigns against people greater
and stronger than Israel. How could Joshua face these difficulties
knowing the odds were against him? He could do so with the courage
that God gave him. Courage always comes from God. It comes from knowing that God is with us in what He has called us to do. When God tells us to do something, he doesn't expect us to walk away from him and then come back when we succeed.

When God tells us to do something, he doesn't expect us to walk away from him and then come back when we succeed.

That's not the way it works. God calls us to do something, and lets us
know that "He is with us" as we put our hands to it. How can we be
afraid when we know God is with us?

My friend and I were driving down the freeway one day because we had received a word from God about going to Seattle. So, when the first exit to Seattle came, we both knew this is where we should go. We ended up parking in an area called Capitol Hill and decided to walk around and talk to people about Jesus. We encountered drug addicts, prostitutes, angry drunk people who made it clear that they didn't want us there, and a whole bunch of other interesting situations. Nothing very powerful happened that day. Actually, I was glad when it was over. Later that week, I was spending some time in prayer when I felt the Lord speak to my heart about going to this same area every week. This was not how I wanted to spend my Saturday, partially because I was afraid. I prayed and asked God for the courage to do what he had asked me to do. In addition to courage, I found such strength as I watched him touch people's lives through us in the weeks following. For the next year or two we spent our Saturdays in Seattle ministering to the homeless, the broken, drug addicts, witches, and even the messed-up religious people.

Many Christians fear that if they really surrender to God, he might tell them to go to some foreign mission field and sacrifice everything for him. This presumption is legitimate. God might call you to *go* just like he did with Abraham, but that is no reason to be afraid. It takes courage to obey God, but we must remember that courage comes from God, and he is always with us.

Chapter 8 Review Questions

1. Have you ever disobeyed God after knowing he has called you to do something? If so, describe the situation. Did you learn from your experience? What will you do differently the next time?

2. Do you struggle with doubt when God speaks to you? Why or why not? What do you need from God in order to move forward with greater faith and confidence in what he tells you?

3. Do you believe that you are fully surrendered to God? Would you be willing to do *anything* that he told you to do at this point in your life? Why or why not? How can you move forward with courage?

4. What encouraged you most about this chapter and how will you apply it to your life?

CHAPTER 9
PURSUING GOD'S VOICE

I was eighteen years old and had just graduated from high school as I excitedly sped into my summer of freedom! Free from school, free from homework—just free, right? Well, not exactly. As soon as the summer began the big question started coming from everybody in my life: "What are you going to do with your life?" At first I had no idea how to respond. Many of the people I knew were going off to university, vocational college, and internships, but not me, because I had no clue what I wanted to do with my life.

During that time I was making incredibly poor choices that delayed my concern for the future and motivation to develop any kind of plan whatsoever. Before long, I started feeling the burden of the big question and knew I needed to do something, so I began looking into colleges and various other opportunities. One day, I found myself in a conversation with a successful web developer, during which he shared with me his passion for his job and the exceptional money he was making. I told him that I thought web design could be a great career path for me, especially after hearing what he had to say. He encouraged me to look into programs at the local community college. Within a few months, I was signed up for a two-year program in web design.

About six months after making the decision to go to school, through a series of incredible circumstances, I gave my life to Jesus Christ and was radically changed forever. Suddenly, all that I thought, all that I was told, and all that I wanted to do was under the review of a new direction—God's direction. I remember going to class, sitting in the back of the room, watching all the eager students, and asking myself, "Why am I doing this?" Seriously. Why am I doing this?" I thought long and hard about why I was pursuing a career path in web design. I quickly realized that I was doing this because a guy told me it would be good for me and I believed him. I was also doing this because I thought this career would provide the most amount of money for the least amount of work—lazy thinking, I know. Suddenly, this thinking didn't seem too good and I really wanted to know what God had to say. I had listened to my web-developer friend, and I had listened to my own voice in wanting to make lots of money. However, I had never pursued the voice of God for my life, so it was time to start fresh. As I began to pursue the voice of God, my constant question was, "God, what do you want me to do?"

We pursue so many things in life based on what others say to us, but as followers of Jesus we should be marked by a pursuit of his voice above all others'. To pursue God's voice means that we consistently ask God for his counsel, direction, and plan concerning our lives. For those who call Jesus their Lord, pursuing his voice in the midst of circumstances, difficulties, and opportunities is the only way. Learning to submit the decision-making process of our lives to God is not always easy, but it is

To pursue God's voice means that we consistently ask God for his counsel, direction, and plan concerning our lives.

entirely essential. I have found that hearing God's voice is not just about hearing him; it's also about the journey of following and depending on him for all things. God is often waiting for us to invite him into the decisions of our lives so that we follow his will and trust that his plan is what's best for us.

In the Old Testament, the nation of Israel had many different kings, but the one who stands out the most is King David. God referred to David as "a man after His own heart," and was honored by God above all the other kings in Israel's history (1 Sam. 13:14). When God said that David was a "man after His own heart," I think he meant that David pursued his heart like none other. The Bible mentions on at least eight occasions that David "inquired of the Lord," which is considerably more than any other king mentioned in scripture. David made many mistakes, committed horrible sins, and in my view was a ruthless individual. But one thing he undoubtedly did right was pursue the voice of God for himself, his family, and the nation of Israel. This is why God honored him above others.

God has never found a perfect person that he can work with, but it seems clear that he is drawn toward those who pursue and prioritize what he says. If we really want to walk in God's will then we can't sit back, passively waiting for him to do or say something. We need to be relentless in our consistent pursuit of what God is saying.

Our Dependence Fuels Our Pursuit

We must recognize that pursuing the voice of God successfully is tied to our dependence upon him. In our sin we separated ourselves from God's voice and began trusting ourselves for direction and answers. In Christ, we reject an autonomous, self-seeking life and re-connect to God in true dependence, wherein we not only want his voice, but also recognize that we need his voice.

Dependence is the state or condition of needing or relying on someone to aid, support, and sustain us. We need God. We need His voice. Without God's voice in our lives, we will believe in the finished work of Jesus for future salvation in the future, but will follow our own voices in our present day. Our actions won't work in harmony with our beliefs, and will lead us to further destruction. Therefore, dependence on God is the fuel for pursuing God's voice in life. We only care what he has to say if we know that we *need to hear* what he has to say.

Jesus's life and ministry exemplifies the kind of dependence on God that we need to have. In Matthew 3 and 4, Jesus begins his ministry at the age of thirty by being baptized and then led into the wilderness by the Holy Spirit. While in the wilderness, Jesus endures a series of temptations during a unique encounter with the devil.

> Then Jesus was led up by the Spirit into the wilderness to be tempted by the devil. And after He had fasted forty days and forty nights, He then became hungry. And the tempter came and said to Him, "If You are the Son of God, command that these stones become bread." But He answered and said, "It is written, 'MAN SHALL NOT LIVE ON BREAD ALONE, BUT ON EVERY WORD THAT PROCEEDS OUT OF THE MOUTH OF GOD.'" (Matt. 4:1-4)

This passage records the first of three temptations that Satan brings to Jesus in his attempt to derail the plan of God. Satan knew that Jesus was fasting so he provoked him to break his fast and prove his identity by miraculously turning rocks into bread. It doesn't seem like that big of a temptation, right? However, it isn't about Jesus eating bread, but about whose voice he is going to obey—the devil's or his heavenly Father's. The devil's tempting of Adam and Eve was exactly the same: a challenge as to which voice they would obey (Gen. 3). Jesus takes his stand against the devil by proclaiming the truth that his Father's voice is what truly sustains him.

I don't think Jesus could be clearer in saying that the way we live should be dependent on what God says.

I don't think Jesus could be clearer in saying that the way we live should be dependent on what God says. Interestingly, Jesus's statement here is actually a quote from Moses (Deut. 8). In this passage, Moses was preparing the nation of Israel to enter the long-awaited Promised Land after forty years of wandering in the wilderness. In his exhortation to Israel, Moses recalls the difficulties of the wilderness and brings clarity to the past season so that, as they occupy the new land that God is giving them, they won't forget their need for God and his voice in their lives.

In the wilderness, the Israelites had no food, no water, and no way to produce what they physically needed to keep themselves alive. God didn't want Israel to starve, but he did want them to learn how to depend on him and not their circumstances. In the wilderness, God sent manna from heaven and told the people how to collect it so they could have food every day (Exod. 16:4), and he also told Moses to throw a tree branch into a polluted body of water so they could have clean drinking water (Exod. 15:22-25). Israel stayed alive because they listened to what God said, which is exactly what Moses wanted them to remember as they journeyed into a new land filled with houses, fields, vineyards, and springs of fresh water.

It is easy to trust in what we have or what we can do, but life will throw us lots of curveballs and the ground will at times shift right under our feet. However, it is my conviction that if we don't have an urgency to hear from God, we most likely won't pursue what he has to say. The great tragedy of God's people throughout history is that we tend to do what's right in our own eyes, not inquiring of God at all; as a result, we go astray. Life is full of "I-don't-know-what-to-do" moments, which should provoke us to hear God, in place of just doing stuff and hoping it works. I encourage you to evaluate what you are trusting in and ensure that you are truly depending on God and his counsel as if your life depends on it, because it actually does!

Our Problem or God's Invitation

Recently, a friend shared with me a current struggle that he and his wife were going through. About five minutes into the conversation my friend said something that, in my opinion, is exactly how Christians should respond to the problems of life: "I am excited to see what God is going to do through this." Think about that response for a second. He didn't ask me what he should do, he didn't ask for prayer, and he didn't even seem stressed out about the problem. He was at peace and excited about what God was going to do in response to the problem. I was greatly encouraged by this conversation and saw clearly how the person who is dependent on God's voice will respond appropriately to the inevitable problems of life.

In Deuteronomy 8, Moses reminded the people of their experience in the wilderness in order to see, specifically, that every problem they had faced over the last forty years of wandering in the wilderness was actually an invitation to pursue the voice of God. This, by the way, is the same passage we just referred to, when Jesus quotes Moses (Deut. 8) while being tempted by the devil in the wilderness (Matt. 4). Let's have a look at it.

> All the commandments that I am commanding you today you shall be careful to do, that you may live and multiply, and go in and possess the land which the LORD swore *to give* to your forefathers. You shall remember all the way which the LORD your God has led you in the wilderness these forty years, that He might humble you, testing you, to know what was in your heart, whether you would keep His command-ments or not. He humbled you and let you be hungry, and fed you with manna which you did not know, nor did your fathers know, that He might make you understand that man does not live by bread alone, but man lives by everything that proceeds out of the mouth of the LORD. (Deut. 8:1-3)

Moses refers to the problems they encountered, specifically not hav-ing food, as something that God allowed so they could learn to ask God and believe him instead of fearing the circumstances. Not only did this teach dependence, as we previously discussed, but it also helped them to see that their problems weren't really problems when they walked with God. Instead, their problems were invitations to pursue God's voice and obey whatever he told them to do.

We must learn that God is not the source of our problems, but rather he is the source of our solutions.

In the wilderness, problems became a source of discouragement to Israel and they chose to complain rather than ask God what to do. I am sure we all have done this at some point: complain instead of ask God. Maybe we still do this. We must learn that God is not the source of our problems, but rather he is the source of our solutions. The problems of life, which are inevitable, become invitations for us to inquire of the one who knows every solution to every problem.

God allowed the Israelites to be hungry so that they would ask him what the plan for food was. The problem, correctly perceived, was actually an invitation. I think we continue to wander around without solutions to our problems because we allow our problems to seem bigger than our God. We tend to get so upset and confused about why something difficult happens that we fail to ask God about it. To stand in our problems and complain that God wasn't there or didn't protect us denies the fact that he is right here ready to lead us through it if we would only pursue his voice and follow him.

While we all encounter problems, some are just the result of living in a fallen world, some are attacks of the enemy, and some are self-induced by our own poor choices; but others are produced by God for his own purposes. Jesus warned his disciples that difficulties would come, but he also encouraged them to be at peace because they were following the one that has overcome all things. "These things I have spoken to you, so that in Me you may have peace. In the world you have tribulation, but take courage; I have overcome the world" (John 16:33). As followers of Jesus we are not promised a problem-free life but we can be sure that God will always lead us through the difficulties as we pursue his voice.

Our problems must not replace our focus on God, and they don't have the right to dictate our emotions if we follow the *one* who knows all things and uses all things for his purposes (Rom. 8:28-29). As we face our own difficulties, we must take a step back and ask the Lord what to do. Nothing takes God by surprise—he always knows what to do and we can always trust where he is leading us.

Pursuing God's Voice through the Bible

While the importance of pursuing God's voice cannot be overstated, we also need to discuss *how* we actually pursue God's voice. As you have heard me say many times, the Bible is the primary way we learn about God and hear his voice. The Bible is always the first place we should start pursuing the voice of God.

It is my personal conviction that every Christian should read and study the Bible every single day. A lot of things that happen in our lives, which potentially draw out questions and or confusion, would be settled quickly in our hearts if we were just devoted to the daily study of God's word. My regular habit is to read three to four chapters of the Bible per day and write out the verses that challenge me or require additional study and contemplation, all of which typically amounts to a page or so in my journal. This regular discipline has become so life-giving that I can't imagine going a day without it. Spending time in God's word is essential to maintaining spiritual health and necessary if we are going to be people who hear God's voice.

While I am devoted to pursuing God's voice through habitually studying the Bible, I have also found that many circumstances require me to dig even deeper in my studies. When we are unsure of what to do in a circumstance, we should automatically go to the Bible to see what God says about it. Granted, there are times when the Bible only answers our circumstances generally, yet it still gives us a basic framework by which we can begin seeking the Lord in prayer.

Think about all of the controversial topics today, even in the church: homosexuality, politics, heaven and hell, dating and relationships, racism, etc. How many of us have truly studied the Bible, for ourselves, on the issues that concern our culture, churches, and families? How many of us have pursued God's voice in the Bible through rigorously studying a matter that we were facing that needs to be addressed with God's mind and not just our opinions?

I can't tell you how many times I have been asked to pray with someone to hear God's voice concerning a matter that is already answered clearly in the Bible. The typical scenario is for someone to ask me to pray that God would provide a new place of employment because the current job is riddled with ungodly people who are unkind. While it may be possible that God would have this person move on for some reason, I think the Bible is clear about what we are to do when people mistreat us. The person will ask me, "What do you think God wants me to do?" with the expectation that I will pray and give a prophetic word, or take a reactionary approach to their mistreatment. In counseling such a person, I always go to the Bible first: "Have you prayed for these people?" The typical answer is "No." If the Bible directly tells us what to do, that is always God's voice for the situation. In this case, we read, "...love your enemies, do good to those who hate you, bless those who curse you, pray for those who mistreat you" (Luke 6:27-28). If we are going to pursue God's voice, we must first let the Bible inform our circumstances, as if God were speaking directly to us, because he is!

If we are going to pursue God's voice, we must first let the Bible inform our circumstances, as if God were speaking directly to us, because he is!

Friends, we are blessed with the amount of biblical knowledge available to us today. The Bible is God's word (2 Tim. 3:16), and contains what he wants us to know, not the mere opinions of men (2 Pet. 1:20-21). This leaves us without excuse when it comes to having God's perspective on most issues in which we need to know the mind of God. If we would take him at his word and pursue his voice, we would have greater peace and a more solid foundation by which to make decisions.

Pursuing God's Voice through Prayer

Alongside the Bible, we are called to pursue God's voice through prayer. I am sure you have heard many different definitions for prayer but let's be really clear: the word pray means "to ask" or "make a request." That's all it means. Too simple, right? Usually when people pray, they ask God to *do* something, which is totally fine. However, before we can ask God to *do* something, we should want to know what exactly he *wants* to do, otherwise we may be asking for something that opposes his will. This is why prayer should primarily be about pursuing God's voice, and secondly about asking him to do things. With this in mind I have written a definition of prayer: "discovering what God wants to do and then asking him to do it."

God always responds to our prayers. King David knew this when he prayed about leading his army into battle against the Philistines. "So David inquired of the Lord, saying, 'Shall I go and attack these Philistines?' And the Lord said to David, 'Go and attack the Philistines and deliver Keilah'" (1 Sam. 23:2). David pursued God's voice through prayer and God answered him, which is the same way it works for us. Remember, God has the answers for everything, but he still wants us to ask him. Thus, those who pray will hear God's voice more often than those who don't.

During a time of transition I began praying about what God wanted me to do. While he had given me peace to quit my job, I had no real direction about what the next thing would be, which is not the way I typically do things. So, I began studying the Bible and writing for several hours a day while I waited for God to provide further direction. The waiting was frustrating because I wanted to know immediately. I was offered a few jobs but none of them felt right until one day when my dad called me and suggested the idea of working with him in real estate. I got off the phone with my dad and immediately received a peace from God that this was his answer to what I had been asking him about. Looking back ten years later, I know clearly that this was the right decision. I am so glad that God answers our prayers when we come to him and pursue his voice in our circumstances.

It's so important that we pray about things before we make decisions.

It's so important that we pray about things before we make decisions. Sure, there are many decisions in life where we don't need a scripture or some word from God, like what movie I'm going to watch tonight. But there are also many things in life that we should be seeking God about instead of just speaking or acting as though we already know what God wants us to do. Can you imagine what David's life would be like if he just went to war without asking God about it? Maybe David would have lost men, his kingship, or, quite possibly, his life. Our decisions should be the result of what God says. Typically, God will speak to us in response to our prayers.

I encourage you to develop a lifestyle of prayer that goes beyond a once-a-day practice. We don't just sit with God once a day; we walk with him all day because he lives in us! I ask the Lord for wisdom before almost every meeting and I also ask him to speak to me about how to disciple my children. The point is that we never stop praying (1 Thess. 5:17) because asking God is more than making a momentary request, it's a lifestyle.

Pursuing God's Voice Through Fasting

Fasting has been incredibly helpful in my pursuit of God's voice. Now I need to be really honest and I am sure you can relate: I really like food. I like food a lot. Fasting is not easy for me. Whenever I hear people say how they love fasting, I tend to think they are blowing smoke or something is seriously wrong with them (note the sarcasm). I don't fast on accident and it's never something that I do lightly, but when I am cloudy on an issue and don't know what to do, I pursue God's voice through the combination of fasting and prayer.

By definition, fasting is when someone abstains from food (or other things) for a specific period of time in order to seek God through prayer. In the Old Testament, God required Israel to fast collectively at least once a year on the Day of Atonement as well as other occasions (Lev. 23:27). In the New Testament, we have records of the early church fasting and praying together as they sought God for his direction (Acts 13:1-2). Reliable church tradition and recorded history also tell us that the early church (post-New Testament) practiced fasting twice a week, usually on Wednesday and Friday.

In my church we initiate a twenty-one-day fast every year on New Year's Day, which we call "Dedicate." The goal of our fast is to set aside the first few weeks of the year in order to hear from God and dedicate the current year to whatever he calls us to do. I have found this to be an incredible time of hungering for God, focusing on his presence, and growing in intimacy with him.

Fasting is mentioned over sixty times in the Bible, and almost every time it's mentioned it is accompanied by prayer. Fasting and prayer go together. Fasting is not some divine diet or twisting God's arm to get him to do something specific. God is a good Father and we don't have to perform religious functions to get his attention. In my opinion, fasting is all about abstaining from the normal flow of life in order to *focus* on God and what he is saying to us. There is so much distraction going on inside and around us that it often takes a physical pulling-away from things and a literal drawing-near to God in order to hear him better.

What greater physical need do we have besides food? As previously examined, in the midst of an incredibly long fast *and* while being tempted by the devil to eat, Jesus

Fasting helps us focus on what is most important: God's voice.

said that what we really need, even more than food, is the voice of God in our lives. Fasting helps us focus on what is most important: God's voice.

There are many different kinds of fasts. This is especially important if you take medication or have complicated physical issues that require a specific diet. Remember, the most important part of fasting is the time spent with God in prayer. If we deny ourselves food and don't spend any time praying then we will accomplish nothing. The following types of fasts are simply references to what we can abstain from while we seek the Lord in prayer. Please take these as suggestions because, ultimately, our fasting is before the Lord and not about making sure we are perfecting the art of some spiritual discipline.

Full Fast

A full fast occurs when someone goes completely without food for a specific period of time. There are at least four references in the Bible in which people fasted food and water. However, I am only referencing food as a full fast for obvious reasons. If you choose to do a full fast, then I recommend you consult with others prior to doing so, especially if you take any kinds of medication.

Partial Fast

A partial fast is to simply go without a meal or two during the day of your fast. For example, you could fast from dinner or lunch and spend an extended amount of time in prayer in place of that meal. There are no rules with this kind of fasting, but you should decide beforehand what you will do and stick with your commitment.

Daniel Fast

This fast comes from Daniel 10, in which Daniel experienced a terrifying vision that caused him to abstain from all pleasant food and drink. Choosing this kind of a fast means that one abstains from all "meats, sweets, and treats." Most people will typically eat fruits, vegetables, and nuts or similar kinds of protein. There are many resources online that provide healthy options for this fast, so I recommend doing some good research.

Media Fast (Daniel 6:18)

Sometimes we are unable to abstain from food for medical or dietary reasons. However, it is still possible to participate in prayer and fasting. I strongly encourage you to fast by replacing some forms of entertainment (TV, movies, internet-surfing) with prayer, Bible study, and intentional devotional time with your family. God often uses this kind of fast to quiet the noises in our lives and to increase our ability to hear his voice.

Ask, Seek, Knock

As we pursue God's voice we need to remember that not everything is automatic. God is God and he knows what to do and when to do it. Our job is to trust him regardless of the circumstances. Sometimes I pursue God's voice in a situation and I hear nothing. Guess what I need to do? Keep pursuing! Look at what Jesus said to his disciples during a conversation about prayer.

> So I say to you, ask, and it will be given to you; seek, and you will find; knock, and it will be opened to you. For everyone who asks, receives; and he who seeks, finds; and to him who knocks, it will be opened. Now suppose one of you fathers is asked by his son for a fish; he will not give him a snake instead of a fish, will he? Or *if* he is asked for an egg, he will not give him a scorpion, will he? If you then, being evil, know how to give good gifts to your children, how much more will *your* heavenly Father give the Holy Spirit to those who ask Him? (Luke 11:9-13)

The people that Jesus shared this with would have understood that the primary point is that those who persist eventually receive. It's easy to get discouraged when you want God to speak to you and, for whatever reason, he doesn't. At this point, before discouragement sets in, we must dig in our heels and continue to pursue God's voice as long as it takes. Jesus promised that those who ask, seek, and knock would eventually receive.

A Life of Response and Pursuit

God is speaking to this generation. Do you hear what he is saying? Are you willing to abandon the comforts, pleasures, and cares of this world in order to bring change to your generation? Will you be added to the list of Hebrews 11 by placing your faith in what God says and acting upon his word? As we hear God in our generation and respond to him with unwavering faith, those who have gone before serve as an encouragement.

> Therefore, since we have so great a cloud of witnesses surrounding us, let us also lay aside every encumbrance and the sin which so easily entangles us, and let us run with endurance the race that is set before us, fixing our eyes on Jesus, the author and perfecter of faith, who for the joy set before Him endured the cross, despising the shame, and has sat down at the right hand of the throne of God. (Heb. 12:1-2)

Pursuing and responding to God's voice is an ongoing process. After God speaks to us we must believe him, obey him, and often endure patiently until he accomplishes what he set out to do. Jesus is the "author and perfecter of our faith" (Heb. 12:2), but we are responsible to pursue God's voice and respond to what he says. Our lives are meant to be one long pursuit of and response to God, as we hear him speak to us regularly all along the way. Since Jesus is the "author and perfecter of our faith," this life begins and ends, rises and falls, in relationship with him. My prayer is that we will have the passion to pursue God's voice and the courage to respond so that our generation will be forever changed!

Chapter 9 Review Questions

1. What does it mean for you to depend on God's voice in your life?

2. When problems occur in your life do you tend to blame God or seek God?

3. What is your daily Bible reading plan? If you lack this commitment, what is your next step to ensure your pursuit of God's voice through the Bible?

4. How will you respond to and pursue God throughout your life?

5. What encouraged you most about this chapter and how will you apply it to your life?

ENDNOTES

1. Vivian S. Park, *The Christian Post: "Scholars Find Decline of Christianity in the West one of the transforming moments in the history of religion worldwide,* http://www.christianpost.com/news/scholars-find-decline-of-christianity-in-the-west-19971/ (March 6th, 2004) Accessed 10/3/2011. Africa in 1900 had 10 million Christians today it has 360 million. According to researcher David Barrett, author of World Christian Encyclopedia, Africa is gaining 8.4 million new Christians a year.

2. Craig S. Keener, *Miracles: The Credibility of The New Testament Accounts* (Grand Rapids, Michigan: Baker Academic, 2011)p.296-297. Keener says that as high as 90% of conversions in China are by healings and miracles.

3. George Barna, *The Last Unregulated Wild Frontier of Influence,* http://www.georgebarna.com/2010/03/the-last-unregulated-wild-frontier-of-influence/ (March 19th, 2010), George Barna also makes the claim that in the United States in the next twenty years, 70% of believers will leave the local church in the United States and will be involved with home churches or some other venue of worship. Accessed 10/3/2013

4. Craig S. Keener, *Miracles: The Credibility of The New Testament Accounts,* (Grand Rapids, Michigan: Baker Academics, 2011), 215.

5. Jon Mark Ruthven, *What's Wrong with Protestant Theology? Traditional Religion vs. Biblical Emphasis.* Tulsa, Oklahoma: Word & Spirit Press. 2011. 3.

6. *NASB Hebrew Aramaic and Greek Dictionaries* (updated edition). 1998. The Lockman Foundation. Hebrew word #5030 for "nabi."

7. *Volume 1, Ante-Nicene Fathers.* "The Apostolic Fathers, Justin Martyr, Irenaeus" (Chapter 5, section "The Martyrdom of Polycarp").

8. *Volume 1, Ante-Nicene Fathers.* "The Apostolic Fathers, Justin Martyr, Irenaeus" (Chapter 5, section "The Martyrdom of Polycarp").

9. *Confessions.* Saint Augustine. Chapter XII.

10. McPherson, Aimee Semple. *This Is That: Personal Experiences, Sermons, and Writings of Aimee Semple McPherson.*

11. *Aimee: Life Story of Aimee Semple McPherson.* 74-75.

12. *NASB Hebrew Aramaic and Greek Dictionaries* (updated edition). 1998. The Lockman Foundation. Greek word #2315 for "theopneustos."

13. *NASB Hebrew Aramaic and Greek Dictionaries* (updated edition). 1998. The Lockman Foundation. Hebrew word #4397 "malak" and the Greek word #32 "aggelos."

14. *NASB Hebrew Aramaic and Greek Dictionaries* (updated edition). 1998. The Lockman Foundation. Greek word #165 "aion."

ABOUT THE MINISTRY

OUR VISION

In 2008 Ben Dixon established a discipleship ministry called "11th Hour Ministries" and later changed the name to "Ignite Global Ministries." Ben is the founder and director of Ignite Global and their vision is to;

- Reach the Nations with the Gospel of Jesus Christ, and
- Strengthen the Church to fulfill the Great Commission

Ben and the Ignite Global team travel extensively throughout the United States and abroad to work alongside churches and ministries to see the lost saved, the church discipled, and everyone empowered by the Holy Spirit to do the works of Jesus Christ.

HOW WE ACCOMPLISH OUR VISION

Practically speaking, we accomplish our vision through regional conferences, our Ignite Discipleship School, training seminars, media resources, and local church partnerships.

Regional Conferences: We regularly host and partner with conferences in multiple locations. These conferences have been extremely fruitful in bringing churches together, equipping believers for kingdom work, and imparting a hunger to see God do greater things.

Ignite Discipleship School: Every year we host our Ignite Discipleship School (IDS) at Mill Creek Foursquare Church. People from all over are invited to take steps into deeper discipleship where we focus on things like how to study the Bible, prayer, hearing God's voice, gifts of the Holy Spirit, evangelism, identity, and serving others.

Training Seminars: We have developed several training seminars that we make available in various locations. Some of the training seminars we have developed include: "Learning to Pray," "Hearing God," "Understanding Prophecy," "Walking in Freedom," "Real Evangelism," "Spiritual Gifts," and "Continuing the Ministry of Jesus."

Media Resources: Through our regional conferences, training seminars, and other gatherings we have developed audio and video resources that are available on our website and other media platforms. In addition to this we have books available as well.

Church Partnerships: It is our goal to strengthen local churches through quality discipleship. This can only happen as we build effective partnerships with churches and ministries for the sole purpose of building up the Body of Christ and reaching the world for Jesus Christ.

GETTING CONNECTED

If you are interested in getting more information about who we are and what we do, please visit us online at www.IgniteGlobalMinistries.org. Also, if you would like to inquire about having Ben Dixon and the Ignite Global team come to your church or event, please send an email to info@igniteglobalministries.org, or call us at (425)-742-3366. We are glad to prayerfully consider how we can partner with you for Kingdom advancement.

 www.IgniteGlobalMinistries.org

 www.facebook.com/Ignite-Global-Ministries-99411582612

 twitter.com/IgniteGlobalMin

 vimeo.com/IgniteGlobal

èGenCo

Generation Culture Transformation
Specializing in publishing for generation culture change

Visit us Online at:
www.egen.co

Write to: eGenCo
824 Tallow Hill Road
Chambersburg, PA 17202 USA
Phone: 717-461-3436
Email: info@egen.co

 facebook.com/egenbooks

youtube.com/egenpub

egen.co/blog

pinterest.com/eGenDMP

twitter.com/eGenDMP

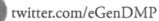 instagram.com/egenco_dmp